Macbeth

A graphic classic by
Trina Robbins

Based on the play by
William Shakespeare

SCHOLASTIC INC.
New York Toronto London Auckland Sydney
Mexico City New Delhi Hong Kong Buenos Aires

Penciller/Layouts
Michael Lilly

Colors, Inks, and Letters
Nimbus Studios

Cover Art
Phil Xavier and Nimbus Studios

Project Management
Greg Waller

Copyright © 2002 Scholastic Inc.
All rights reserved. Published by Scholastic Inc.
Printed in the U.S.A.

ISBN 0-439-12341-0
(meets NASTA specifications)

SCHOLASTIC, READ 180, and associated logos and designs are trademarks and/or registered trademarks of Scholastic Inc.
LEXILE is a trademark of MetaMetrics, Inc.

1 2 3 4 5 6 7 8 9 10   23   10 09 08 07 06 05 04 03 02

WilliaM Shakespeare
(1564–1616)

The most famous writer in the English language lived about 400 years ago. William Shakespeare was an actor and a playwright who is still known and celebrated for his 37 plays and 159 poems. One of Shakespeare's bloodiest plays is the one you're about to read—*Macbeth*.

Reading Shakespeare is an adventure, and part of that adventure is the language. English has changed quite a lot since Shakespeare's day. That's why you'll find a list of *"Words Thou Shouldst Know"* on page 6. Also, whenever you come across words in italics (*like these*), flip to the back of the book and find out *"What Shakespeare Was Saying."*

Macbeth's World

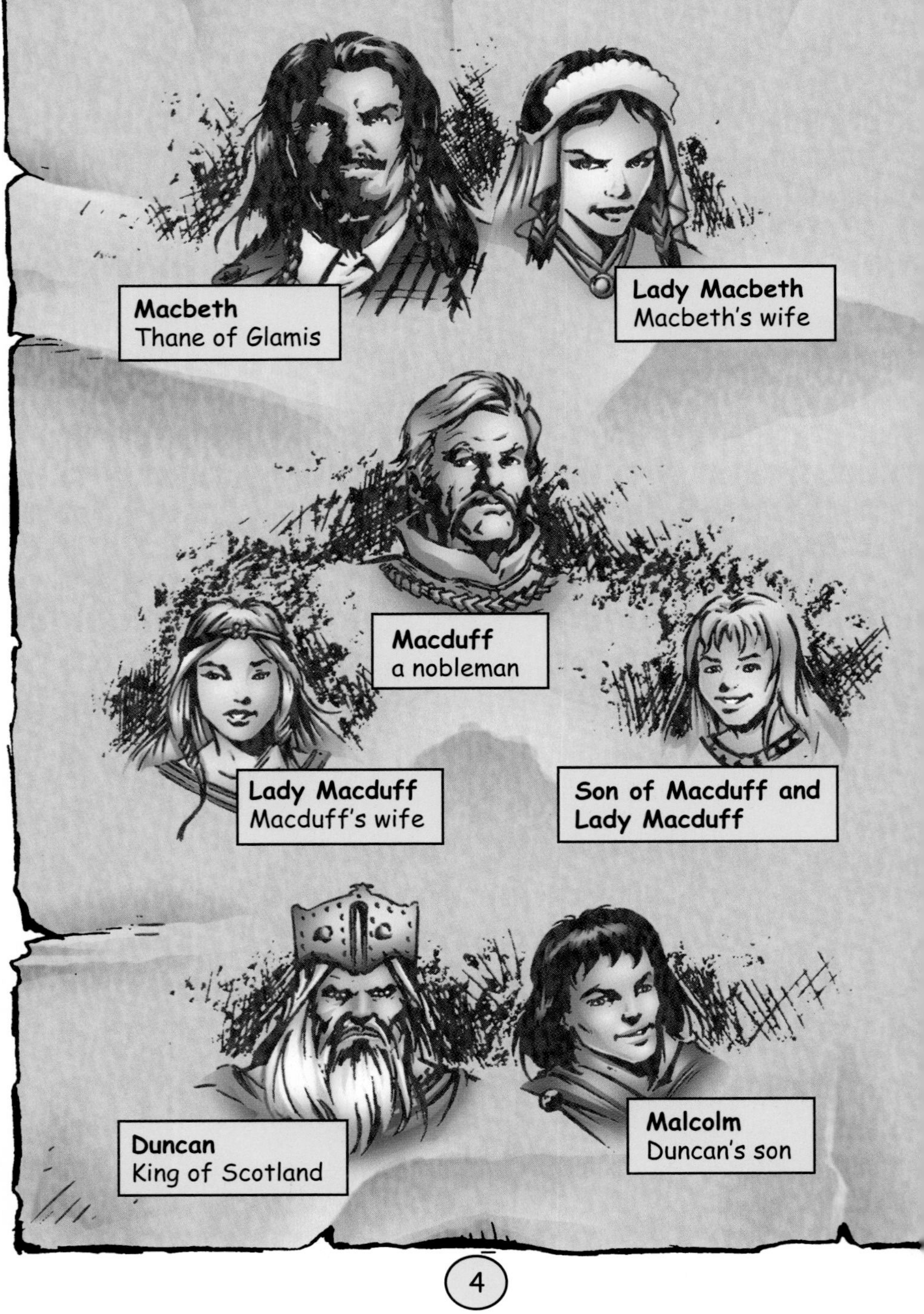
Macbeth
Thane of Glamis
Lady Macbeth
Macbeth's wife
Macduff
a nobleman
Lady Macduff
Macduff's wife
Son of Macduff and Lady Macduff
Duncan
King of Scotland
Malcolm
Duncan's son

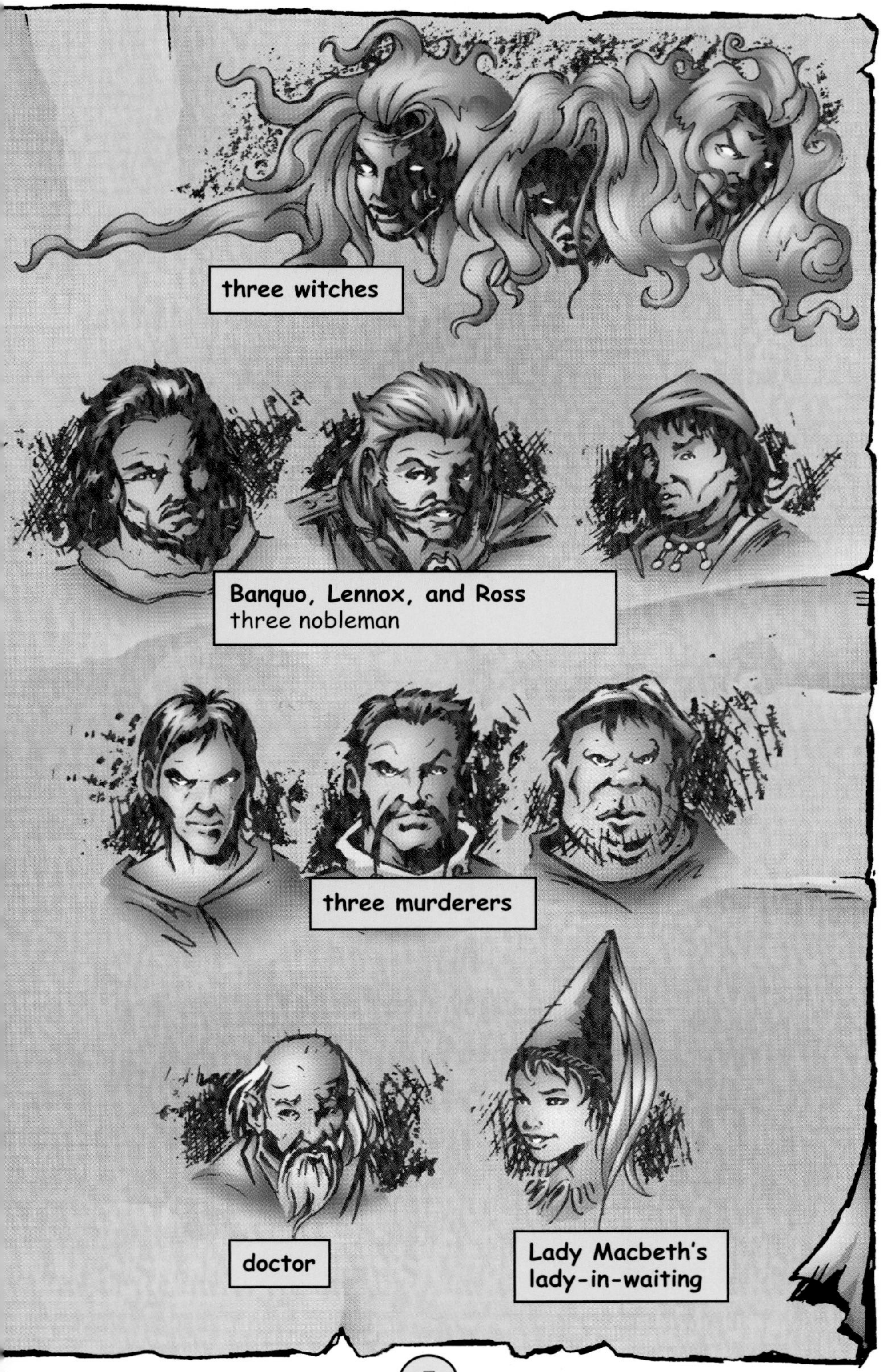
three witches
Banquo, Lennox, and Ross
three nobleman
three murderers
doctor
Lady Macbeth's
lady-in-waiting

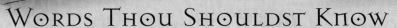

Words Thou Shouldst Know

Shakespeare wrote in English. But let's face it. Sometimes it doesn't look like it.

That's because the language has changed a lot over the past 400 years. And many words that were common in Shakespeare's day are no longer used—though, sometimes, they *do* sort of look familiar.

Here's a list of words that appear often in Shakespeare. Get to know them before you start the story.

art = are	hereafter = after this
aye = yes	shalt = will
canst = can	thane = lord
bade = told	thee = you
didst = did	thou = you
doth = does	thy = your
hail = salute	'tis = it is
hast = has	whither = where
hath = has	wilt = will

wᵐ Shakespeare

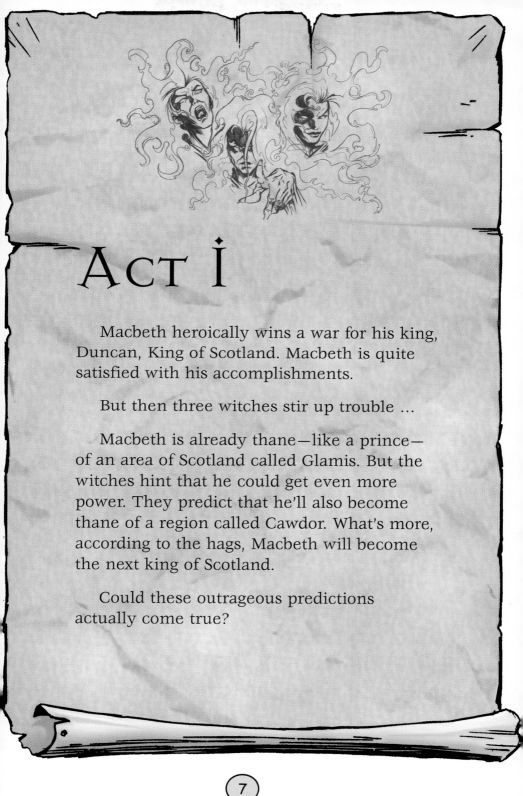

ACT I

Macbeth heroically wins a war for his king, Duncan, King of Scotland. Macbeth is quite satisfied with his accomplishments.

But then three witches stir up trouble ...

Macbeth is already thane—like a prince—of an area of Scotland called Glamis. But the witches hint that he could get even more power. They predict that he'll also become thane of a region called Cawdor. What's more, according to the hags, Macbeth will become the next king of Scotland.

Could these outrageous predictions actually come true?

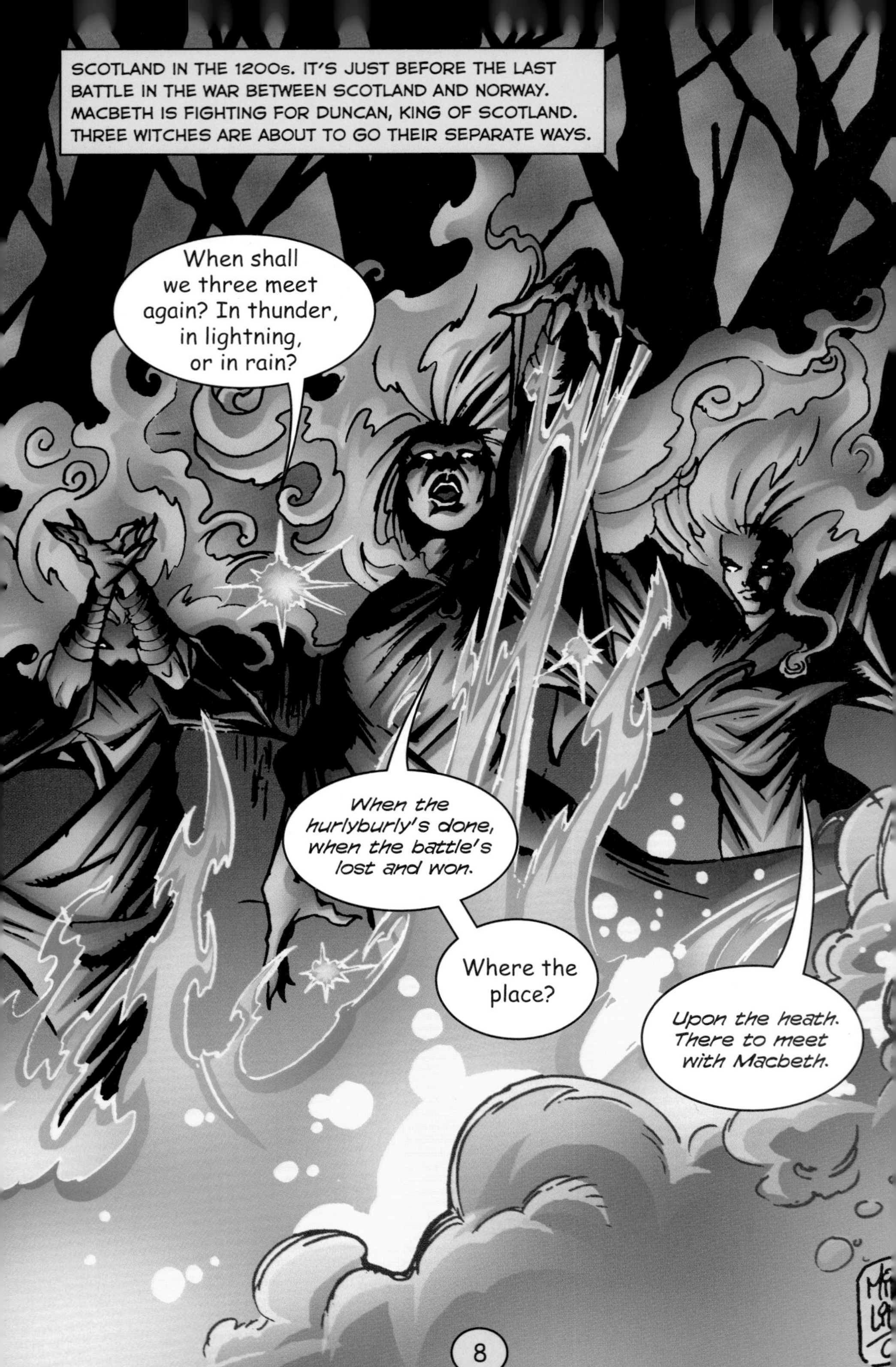
SCOTLAND IN THE 1200s. IT'S JUST BEFORE THE LAST BATTLE IN THE WAR BETWEEN SCOTLAND AND NORWAY. MACBETH IS FIGHTING FOR DUNCAN, KING OF SCOTLAND. THREE WITCHES ARE ABOUT TO GO THEIR SEPARATE WAYS.
When shall we three meet again? In thunder, in lightning, or in rain?
When the hurlyburly's done, when the battle's lost and won.
Where the place?
Upon the heath. There to meet with Macbeth.

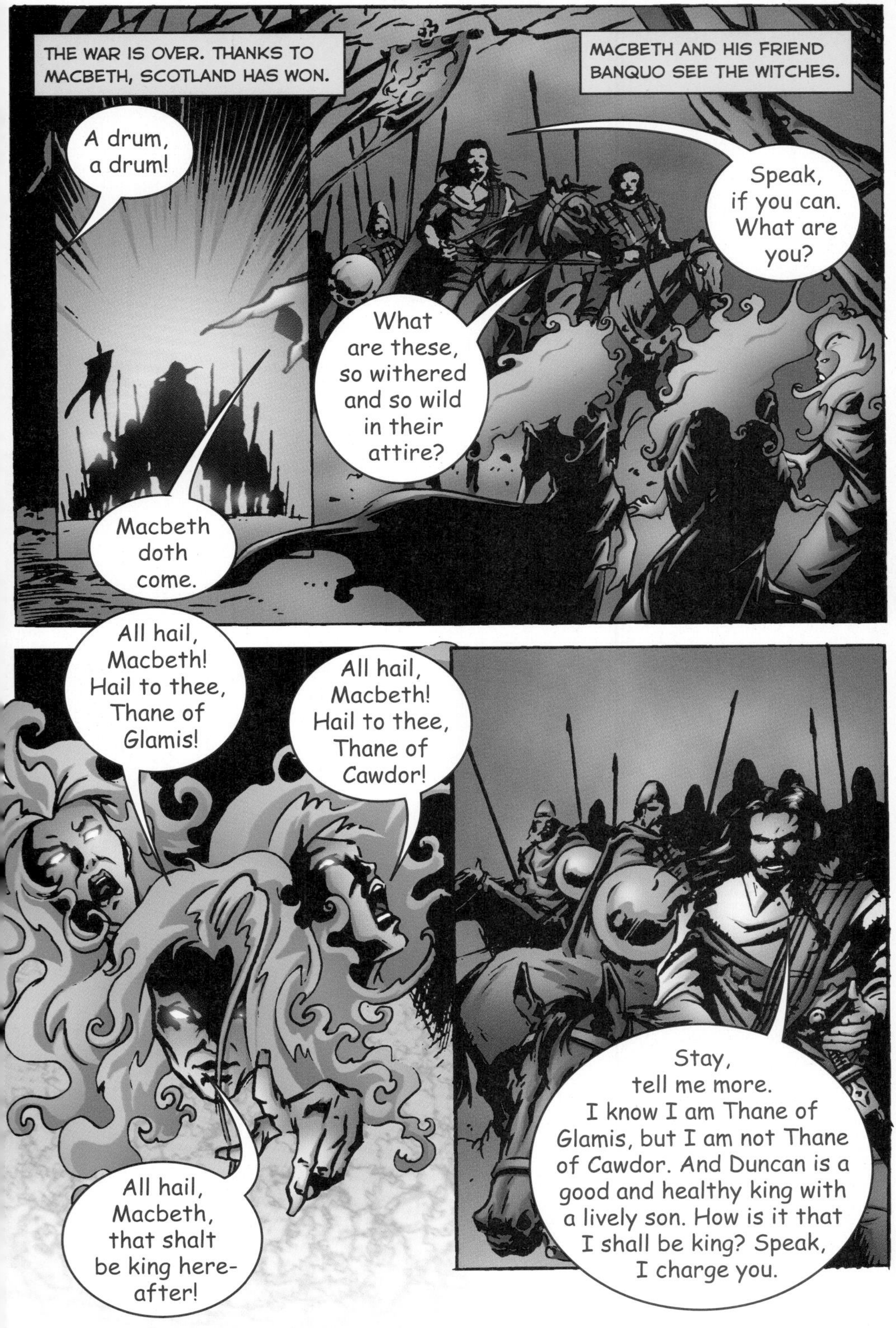
THE WAR IS OVER. THANKS TO MACBETH, SCOTLAND HAS WON.
A drum, a drum!
Macbeth doth come.
MACBETH AND HIS FRIEND BANQUO SEE THE WITCHES.
What are these, so withered and so wild in their attire?
Speak, if you can. What are you?
All hail, Macbeth! Hail to thee, Thane of Glamis!
All hail, Macbeth! Hail to thee, Thane of Cawdor!
All hail, Macbeth, that shalt be king hereafter!
Stay, tell me more. I know I am Thane of Glamis, but I am not Thane of Cawdor. And Duncan is a good and healthy king with a lively son. How is it that I shall be king? Speak, I charge you.

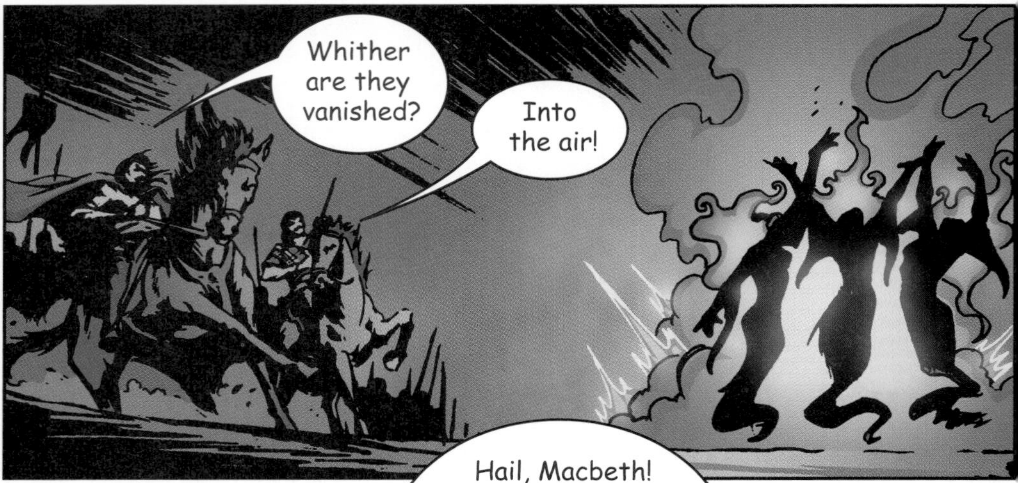
Whither are they vanished?
Into the air!

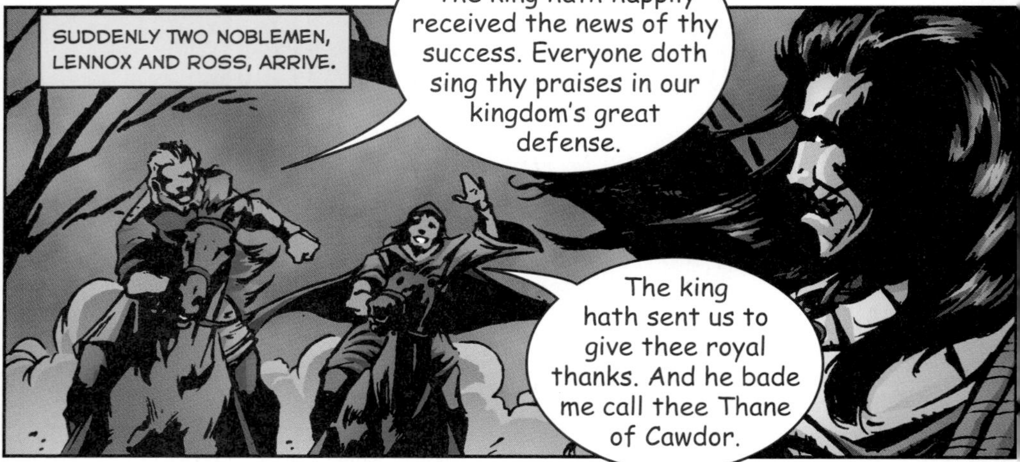
SUDDENLY TWO NOBLEMEN, LENNOX AND ROSS, ARRIVE.
Hail, Macbeth! The king hath happily received the news of thy success. Everyone doth sing thy praises in our kingdom's great defense.
The king hath sent us to give thee royal thanks. And he bade me call thee Thane of Cawdor.

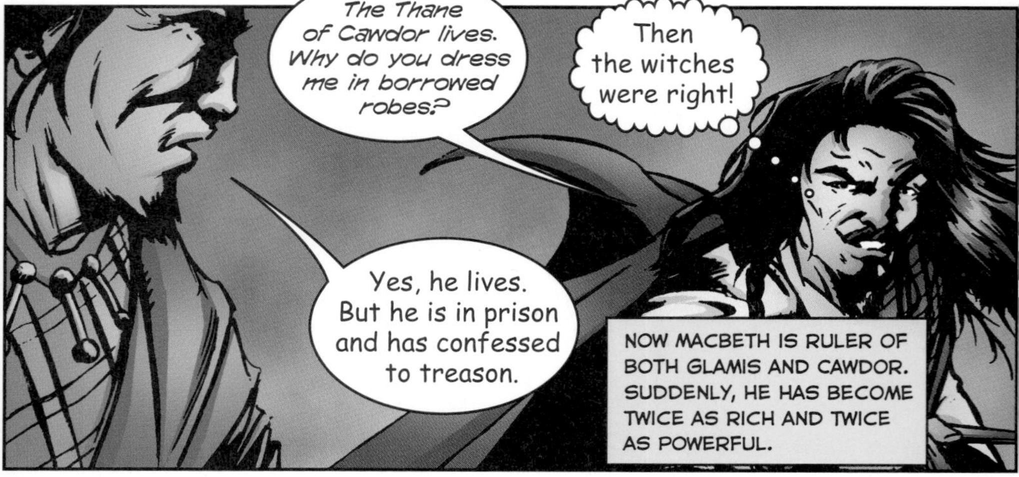
The Thane of Cawdor lives. Why do you dress me in borrowed robes?
Then the witches were right!
Yes, he lives. But he is in prison and has confessed to treason.
NOW MACBETH IS RULER OF BOTH GLAMIS AND CAWDOR. SUDDENLY, HE HAS BECOME TWICE AS RICH AND TWICE AS POWERFUL.

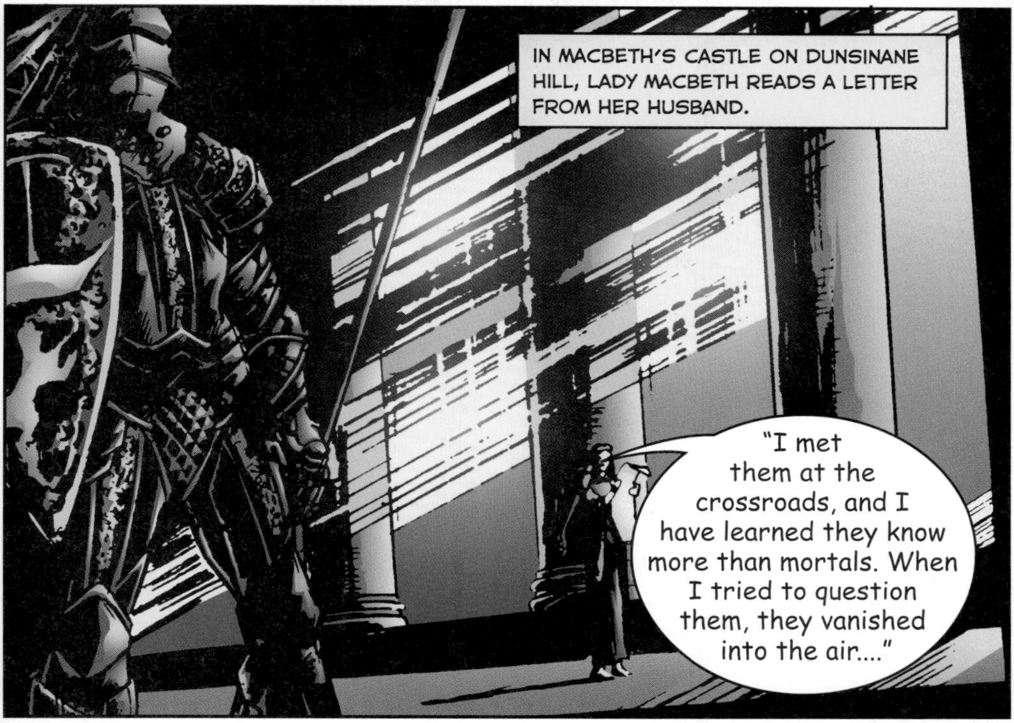
IN MACBETH'S CASTLE ON DUNSINANE HILL, LADY MACBETH READS A LETTER FROM HER HUSBAND.
"I met them at the crossroads, and I have learned they know more than mortals. When I tried to question them, they vanished into the air...."

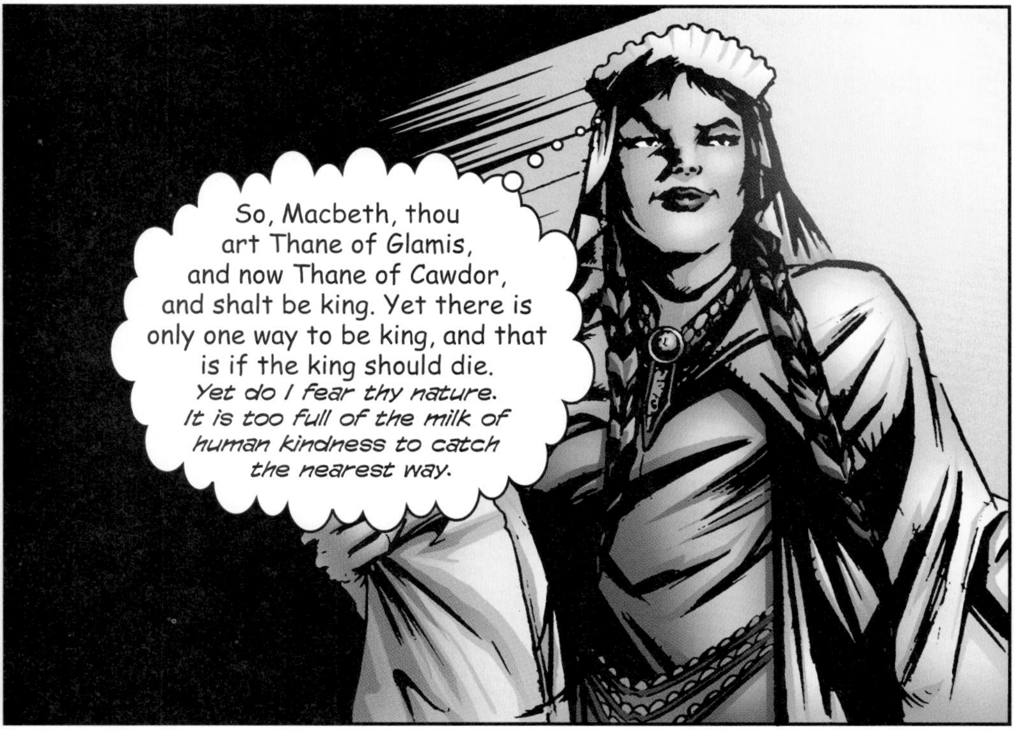
So, Macbeth, thou art Thane of Glamis, and now Thane of Cawdor, and shalt be king. Yet there is only one way to be king, and that is if the king should die. *Yet do I fear thy nature. It is too full of the milk of human kindness to catch the nearest way.*

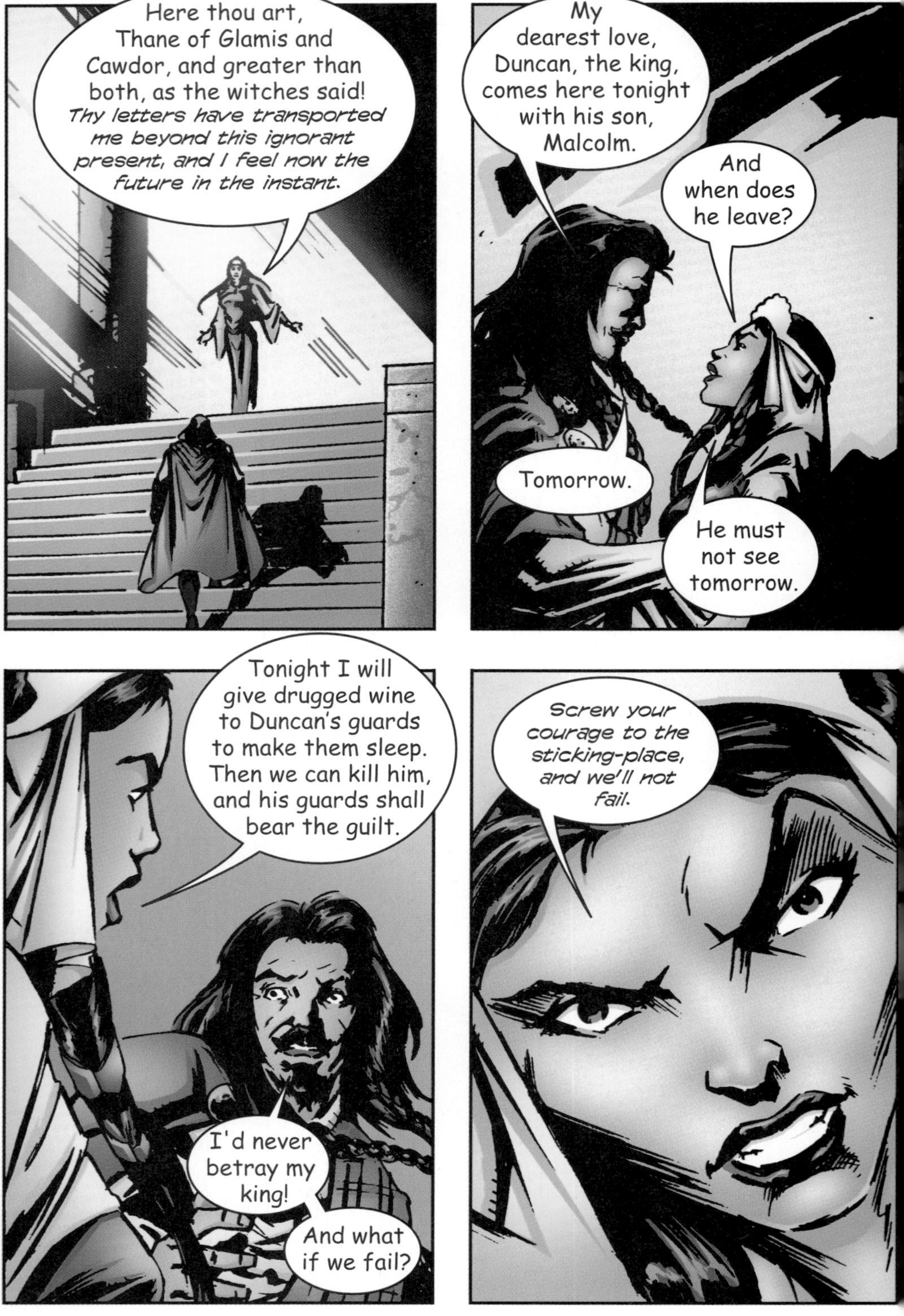

Here thou art, Thane of Glamis and Cawdor, and greater than both, as the witches said! Thy letters have transported me beyond this ignorant present, and I feel now the future in the instant.
My dearest love, Duncan, the king, comes here tonight with his son, Malcolm.
And when does he leave?
Tomorrow.
He must not see tomorrow.
Tonight I will give drugged wine to Duncan's guards to make them sleep. Then we can kill him, and his guards shall bear the guilt.
I'd never betray my king!
And what if we fail?
Screw your courage to the sticking-place, and we'll not fail.

ACT II

Already one of the witches' predictions has come true. Macbeth is now Thane of both Glamis and Cawdor.

Now Lady Macbeth is eager for the next prediction to come true—for Macbeth to become king. She has urged her husband to murder Duncan.

Will Macbeth, who has loyally served Duncan in the war, now turn against him? Or is Macbeth, as his wife fears, too decent to commit murder?

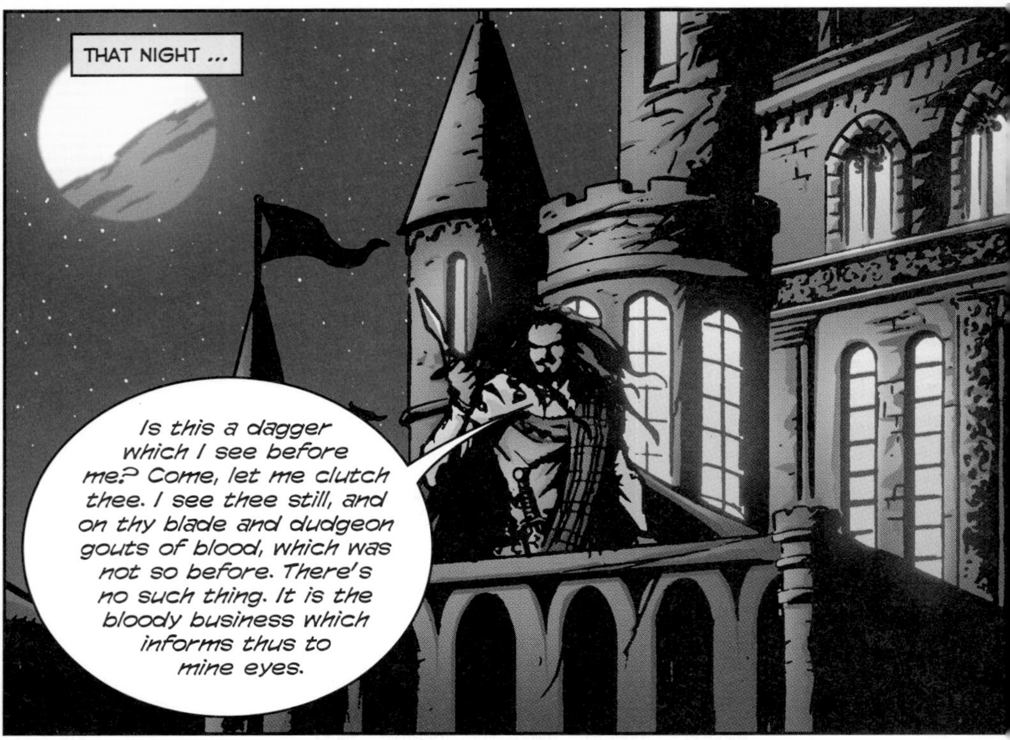
THAT NIGHT ...
Is this a dagger which I see before me? Come, let me clutch thee. I see thee still, and on thy blade and dudgeon gouts of blood, which was not so before. There's no such thing. It is the bloody business which informs thus to mine eyes.

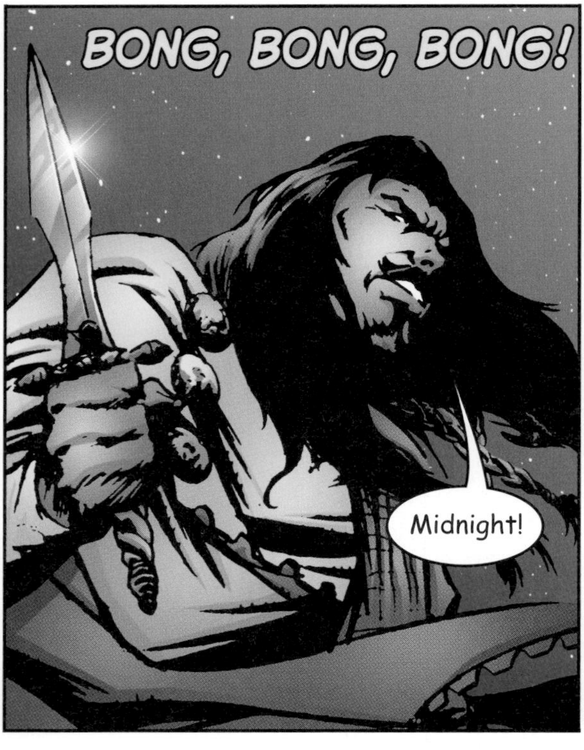
BONG, BONG, BONG!
Midnight!

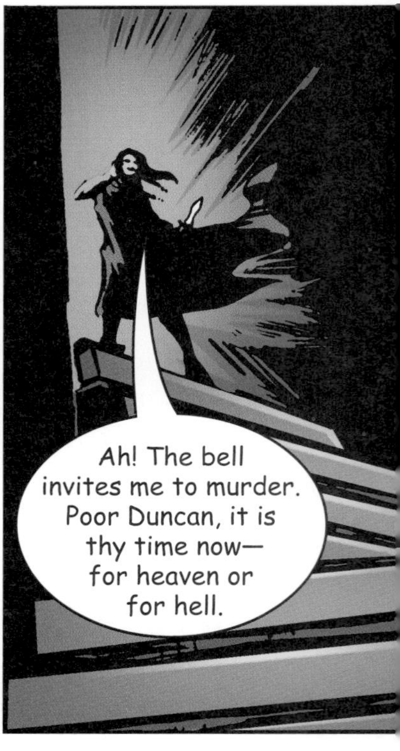
Ah! The bell invites me to murder. Poor Duncan, it is thy time now— for heaven or for hell.

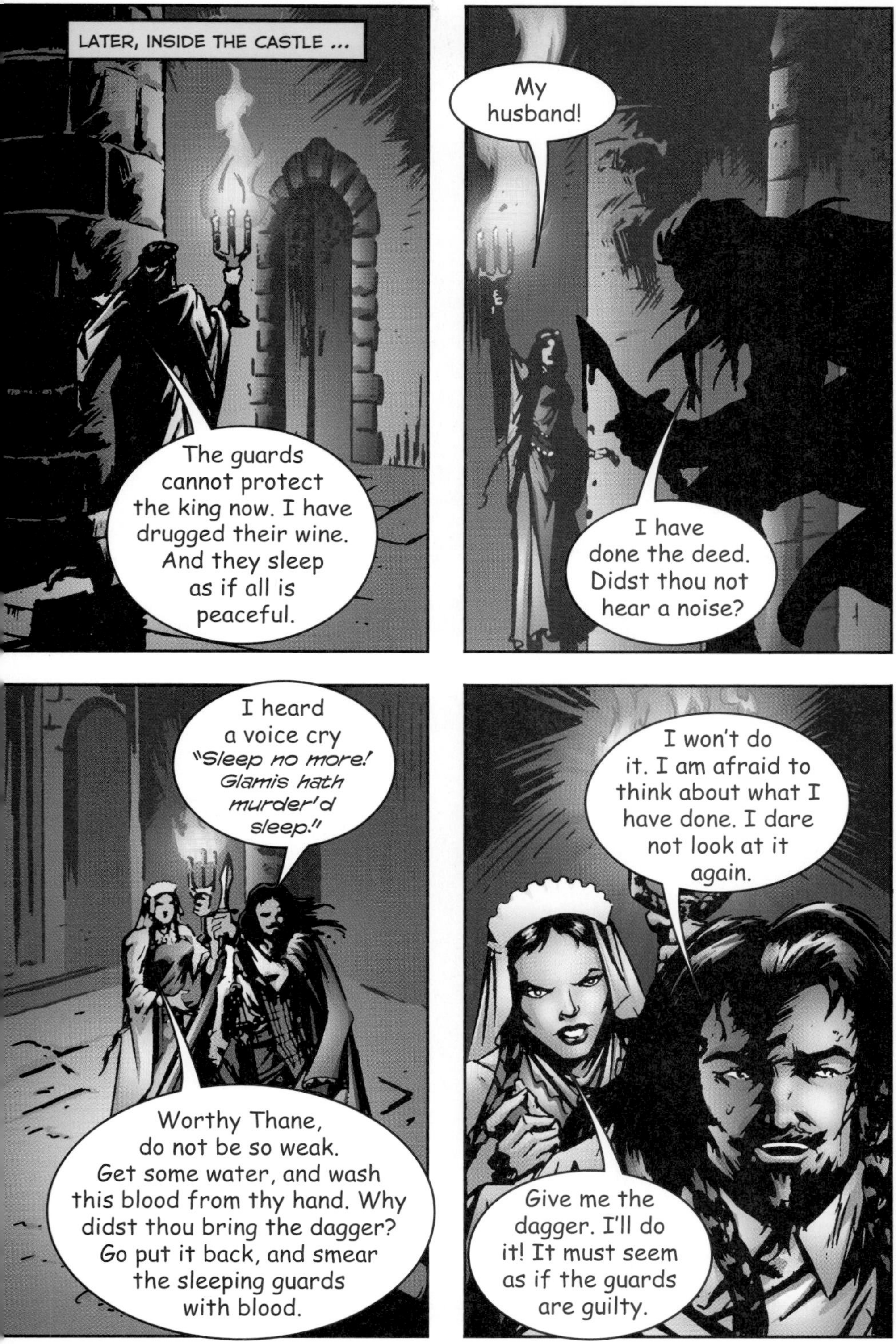
LATER, INSIDE THE CASTLE ...
The guards cannot protect the king now. I have drugged their wine. And they sleep as if all is peaceful.
My husband!
I have done the deed. Didst thou not hear a noise?
I heard a voice cry "Sleep no more! Glamis hath murder'd sleep."
Worthy Thane, do not be so weak. Get some water, and wash this blood from thy hand. Why didst thou bring the dagger? Go put it back, and smear the sleeping guards with blood.
I won't do it. I am afraid to think about what I have done. I dare not look at it again.
Give me the dagger. I'll do it! It must seem as if the guards are guilty.

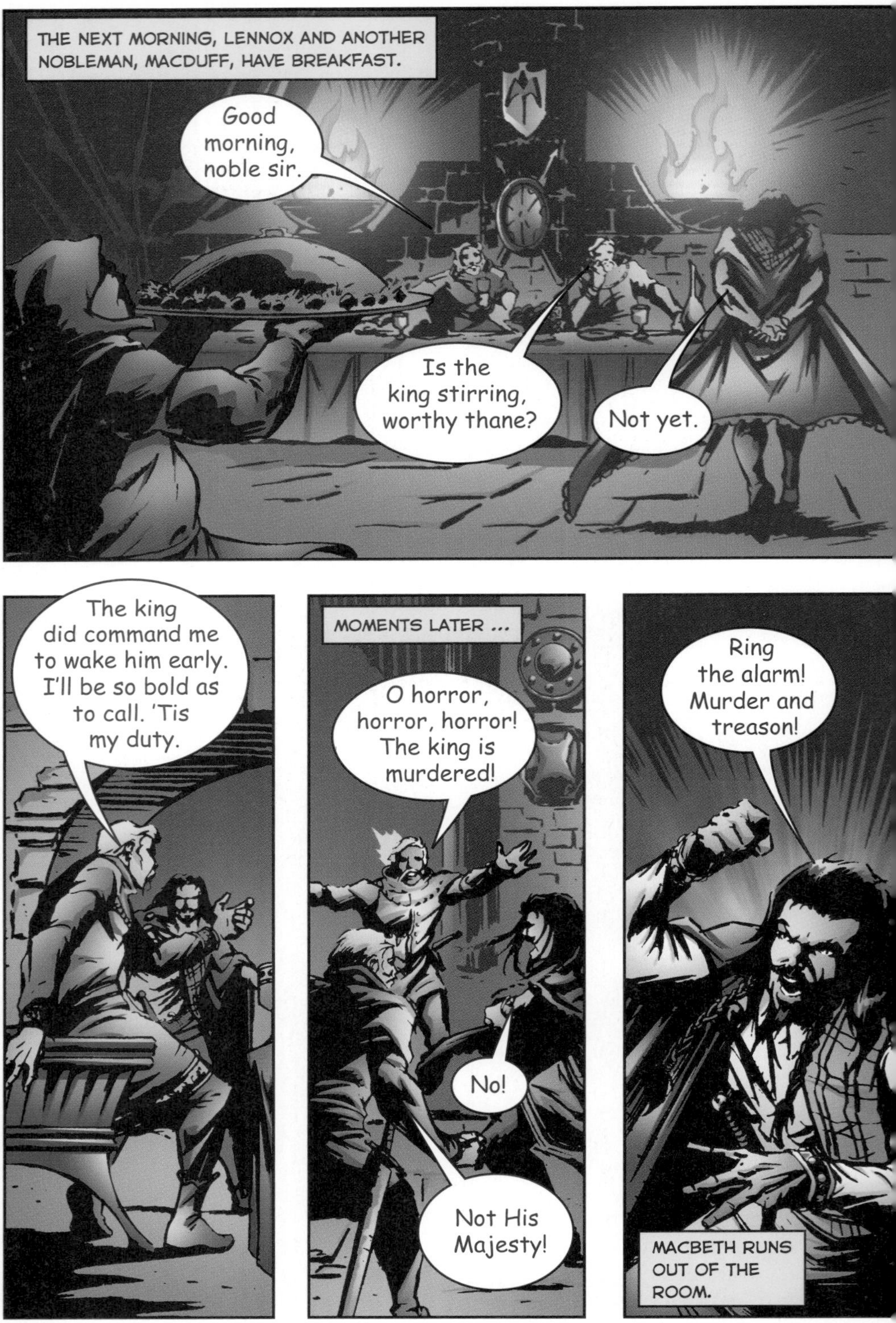
THE NEXT MORNING, LENNOX AND ANOTHER NOBLEMAN, MACDUFF, HAVE BREAKFAST.
Good morning, noble sir.
Is the king stirring, worthy thane?
Not yet.
The king did command me to wake him early. I'll be so bold as to call. 'Tis my duty.
MOMENTS LATER ...
O horror, horror, horror! The king is murdered!
No!
Not His Majesty!
Ring the alarm! Murder and treason!
MACBETH RUNS OUT OF THE ROOM.

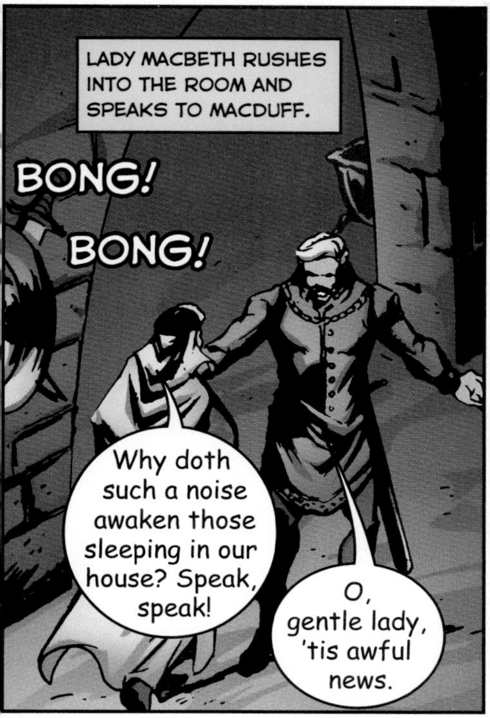
LADY MACBETH RUSHES INTO THE ROOM AND SPEAKS TO MACDUFF.
BONG!
BONG!
Why doth such a noise awaken those sleeping in our house? Speak, speak!
O, gentle lady, 'tis awful news.

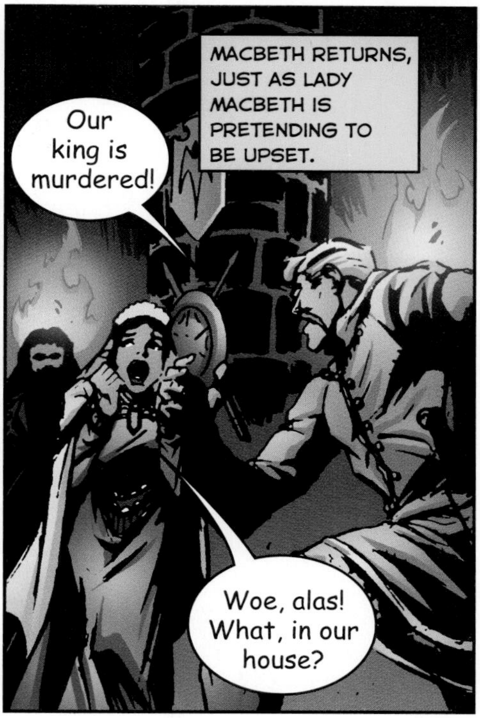
MACBETH RETURNS, JUST AS LADY MACBETH IS PRETENDING TO BE UPSET.
Our king is murdered!
Woe, alas! What, in our house?

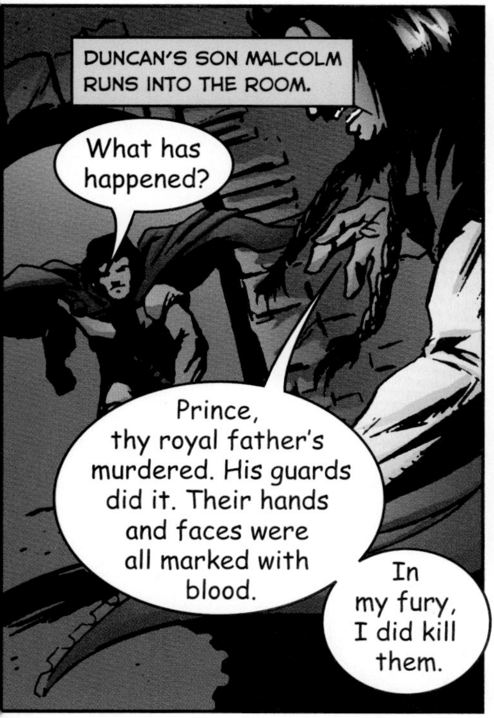
DUNCAN'S SON MALCOLM RUNS INTO THE ROOM.
What has happened?
Prince, thy royal father's murdered. His guards did it. Their hands and faces were all marked with blood.
In my fury, I did kill them.

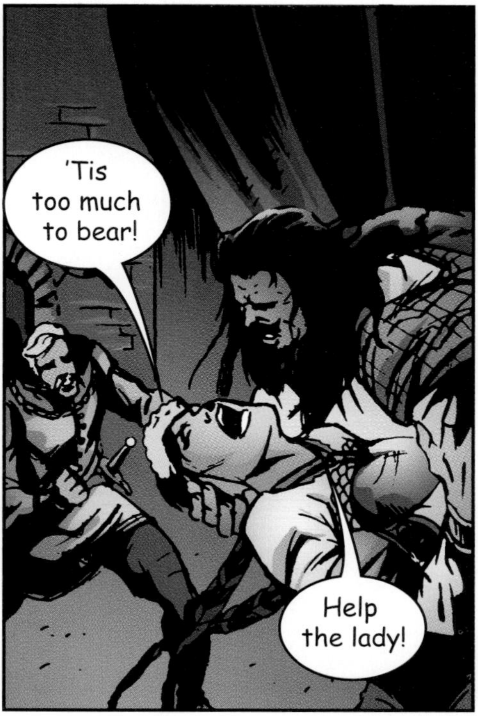
'Tis too much to bear!
Help the lady!

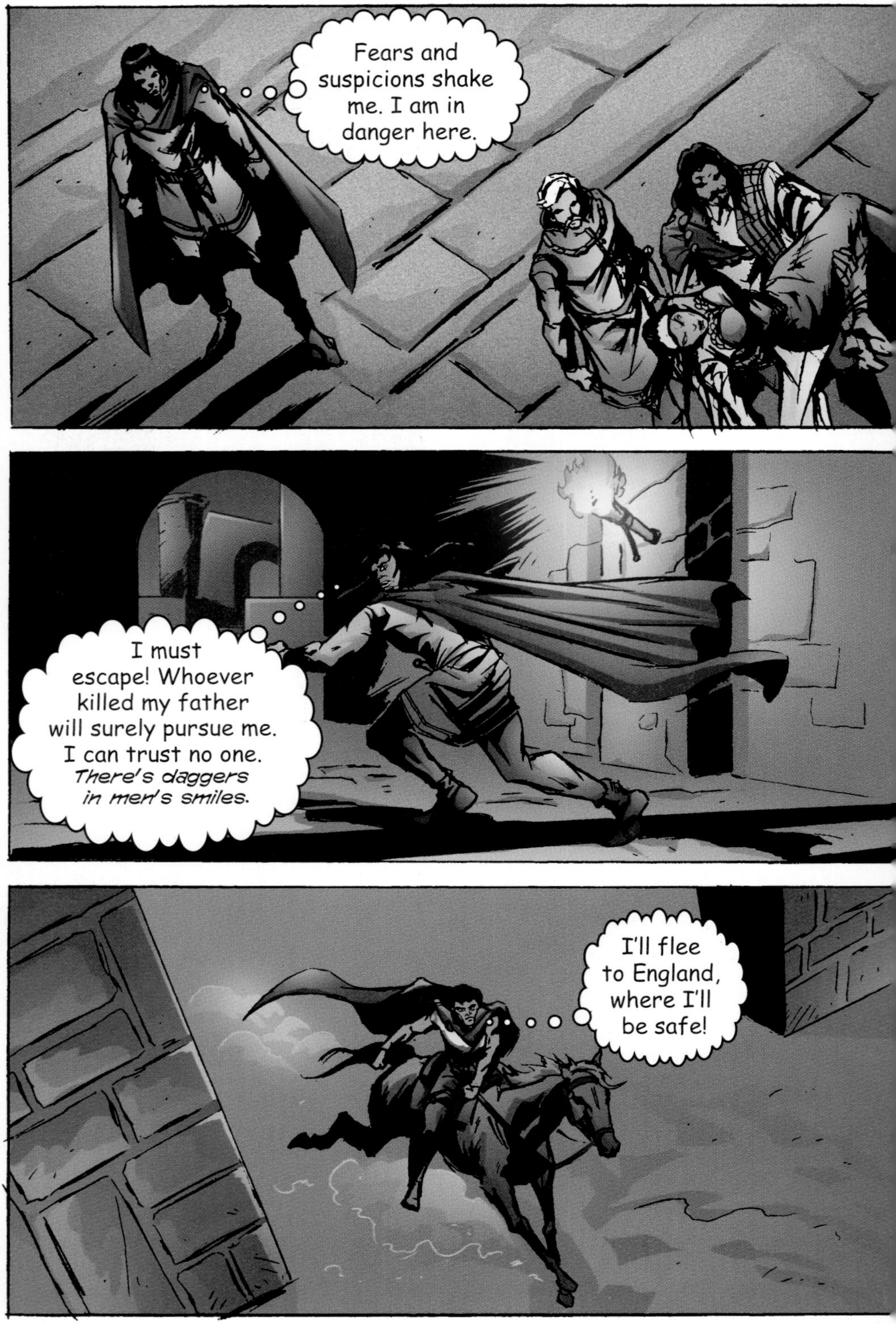
Fears and suspicions shake me. I am in danger here.
I must escape! Whoever killed my father will surely pursue me. I can trust no one. *There's daggers in men's smiles.*
I'll flee to England, where I'll be safe!

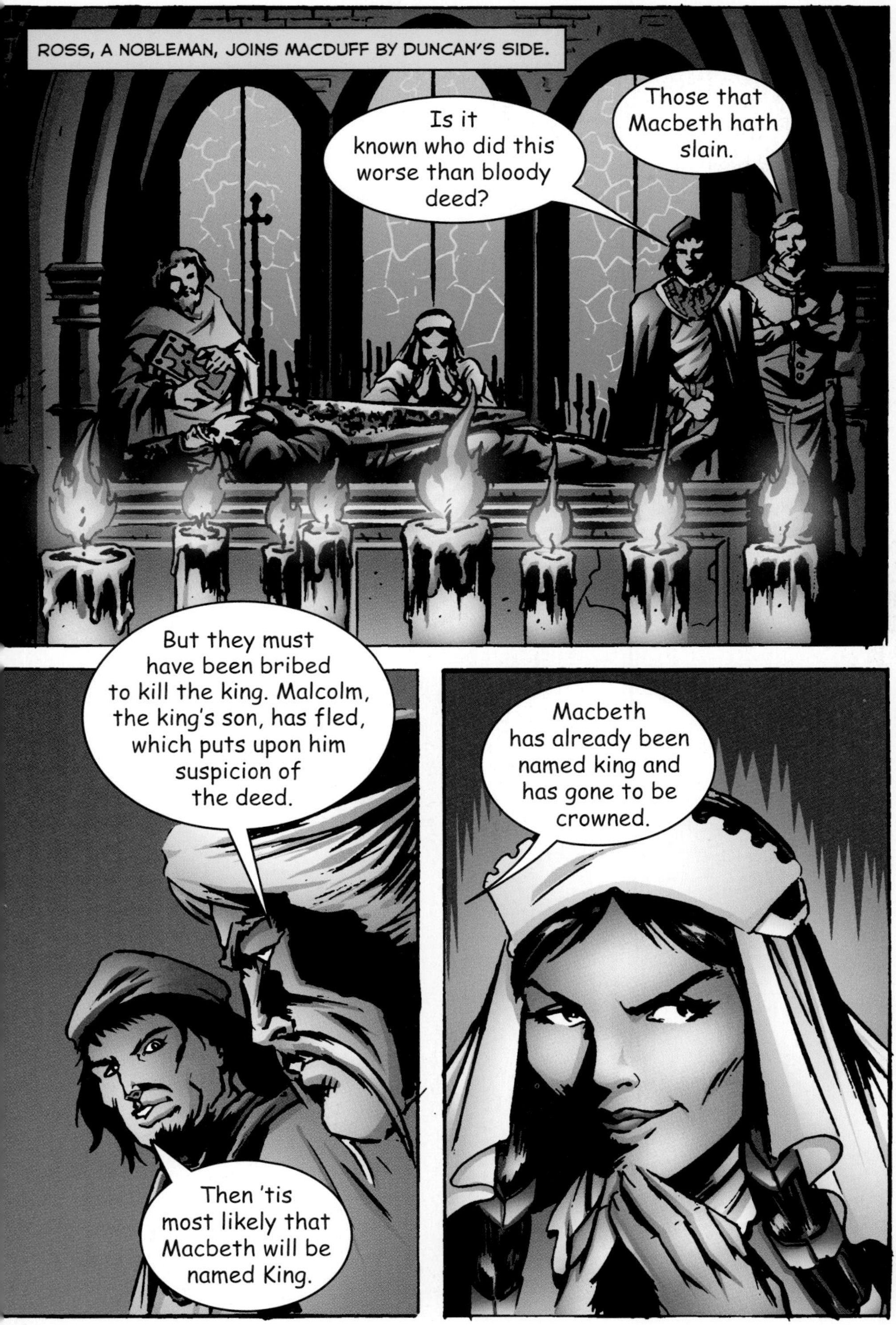
ROSS, A NOBLEMAN, JOINS MACDUFF BY DUNCAN'S SIDE.
Is it known who did this worse than bloody deed?
Those that Macbeth hath slain.
But they must have been bribed to kill the king. Malcolm, the king's son, has fled, which puts upon him suspicion of the deed.
Then 'tis most likely that Macbeth will be named King.
Macbeth has already been named king and has gone to be crowned.

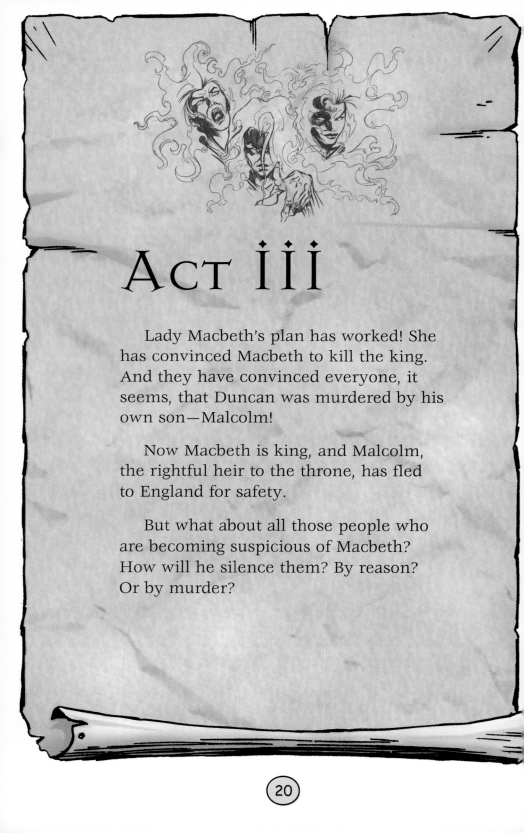

ACT III

Lady Macbeth's plan has worked! She has convinced Macbeth to kill the king. And they have convinced everyone, it seems, that Duncan was murdered by his own son—Malcolm!

Now Macbeth is king, and Malcolm, the rightful heir to the throne, has fled to England for safety.

But what about all those people who are becoming suspicious of Macbeth? How will he silence them? By reason? Or by murder?

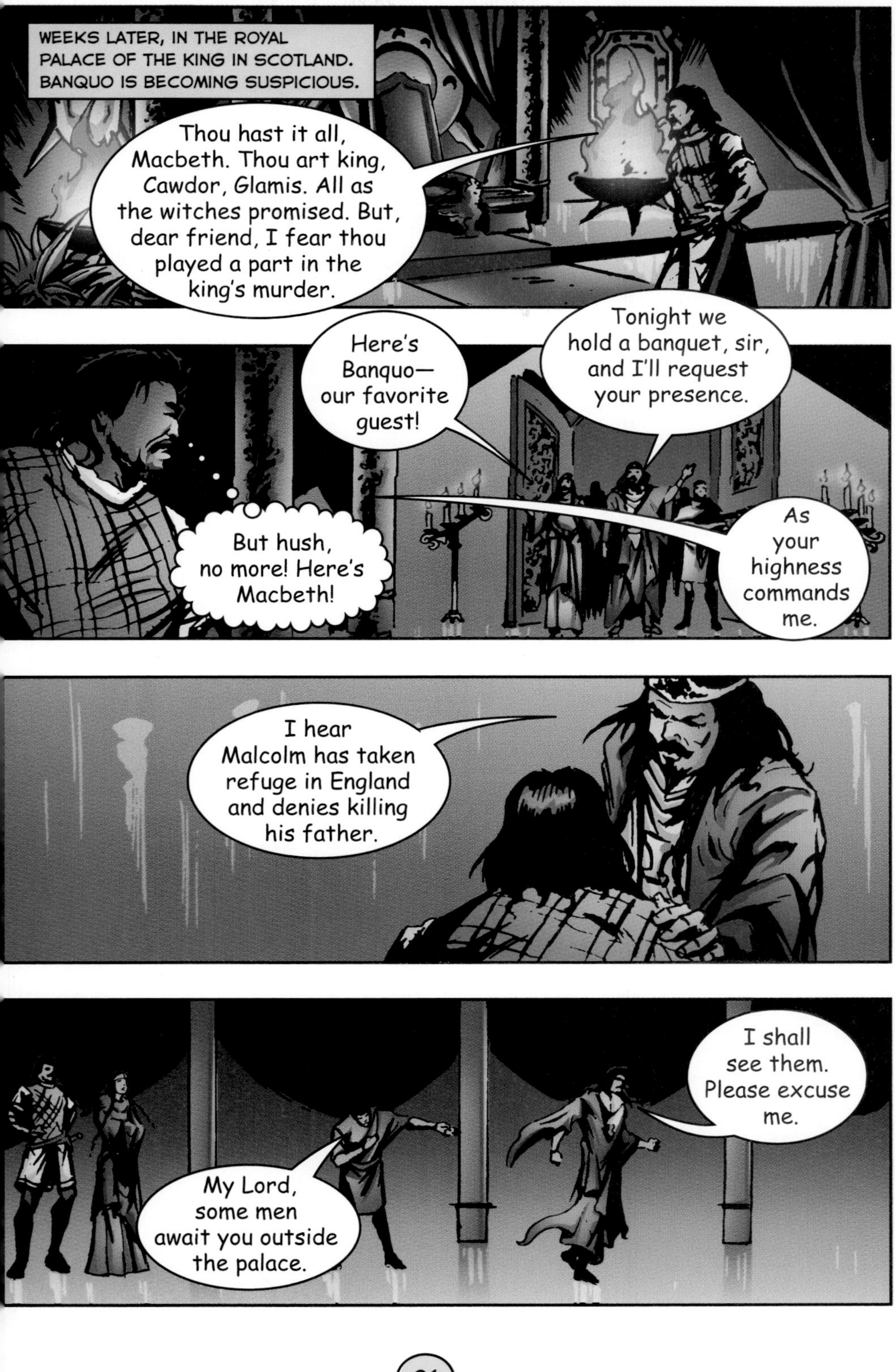
WEEKS LATER, IN THE ROYAL PALACE OF THE KING IN SCOTLAND. BANQUO IS BECOMING SUSPICIOUS.
Thou hast it all, Macbeth. Thou art king, Cawdor, Glamis. All as the witches promised. But, dear friend, I fear thou played a part in the king's murder.
But hush, no more! Here's Macbeth!
Here's Banquo— our favorite guest!
Tonight we hold a banquet, sir, and I'll request your presence.
As your highness commands me.
I hear Malcolm has taken refuge in England and denies killing his father.
My Lord, some men await you outside the palace.
I shall see them. Please excuse me.

Long have I feared Banquo. He knows too much. He was with me when the witches spoke, and I know he suspects me of the King's death. It is time to do something about it.
So here you are. Was it not yesterday we spoke together?
It was, so please Your Highness.
All of you know Banquo is your enemy.
True, my lord.
So he is also my enemy, and every minute of his being is like a knife in my heart. Although, as king, I could crush him, yet I must not, because he has too many friends. Thus it is that I come to you for assistance, keeping this a secret from everyone else.
We shall, my lord, perform what you command us.
It is concluded: Banquo, thy soul's flight, if it find heaven, must find it tonight.

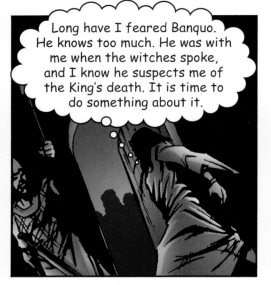

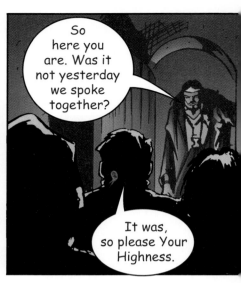

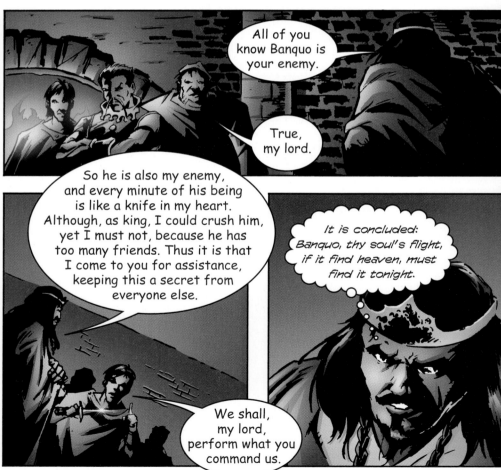

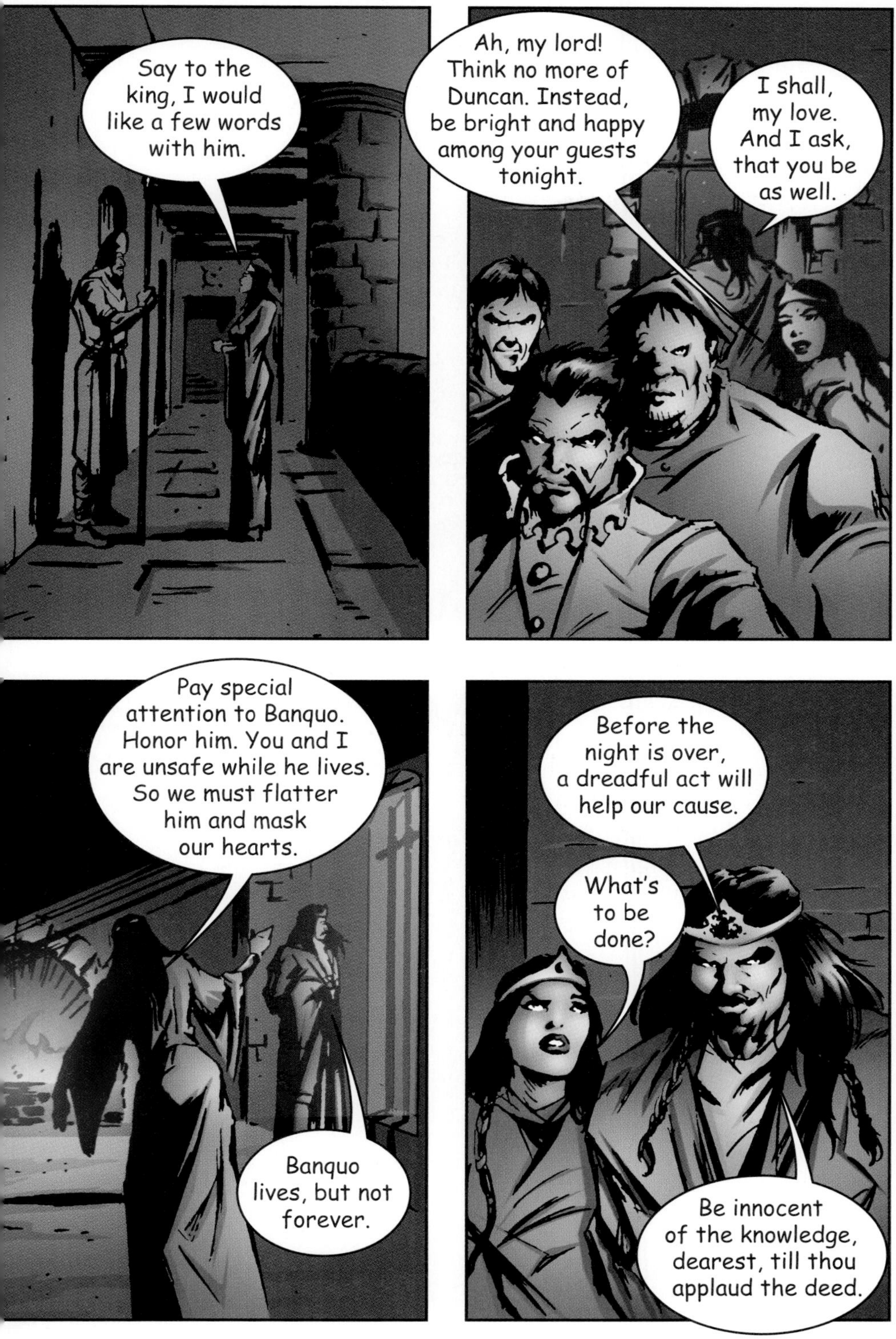
Say to the king, I would like a few words with him.
Ah, my lord! Think no more of Duncan. Instead, be bright and happy among your guests tonight.
I shall, my love. And I ask, that you be as well.
Pay special attention to Banquo. Honor him. You and I are unsafe while he lives. So we must flatter him and mask our hearts.
Banquo lives, but not forever.
Before the night is over, a dreadful act will help our cause.
What's to be done?
Be innocent of the knowledge, dearest, till thou applaud the deed.

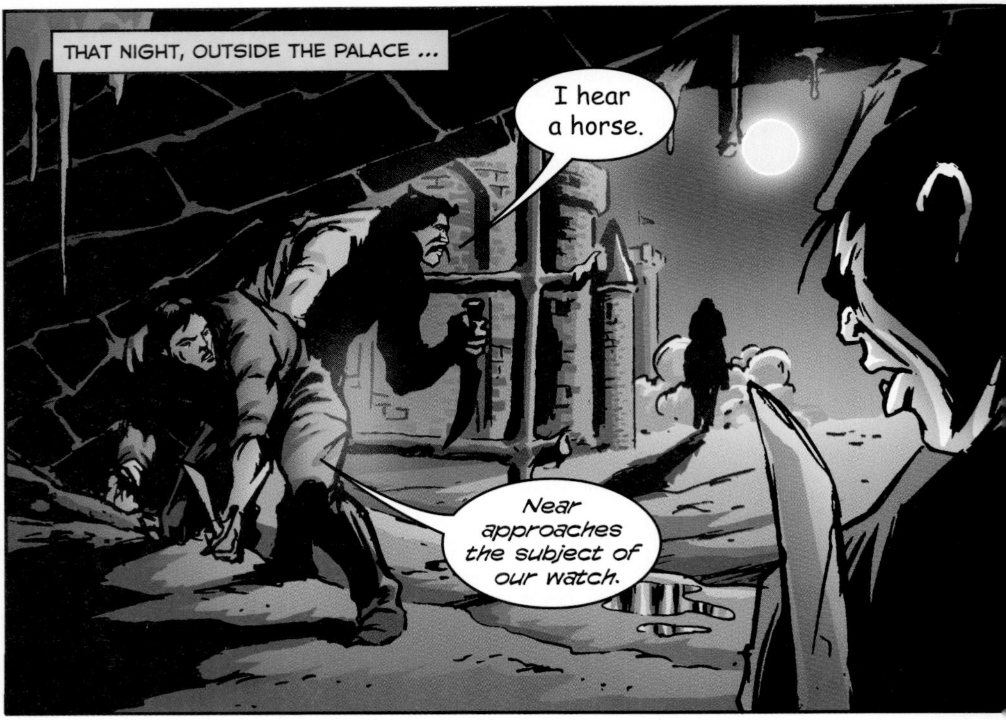
THAT NIGHT, OUTSIDE THE PALACE ...
I hear a horse.
Near approaches the subject of our watch.

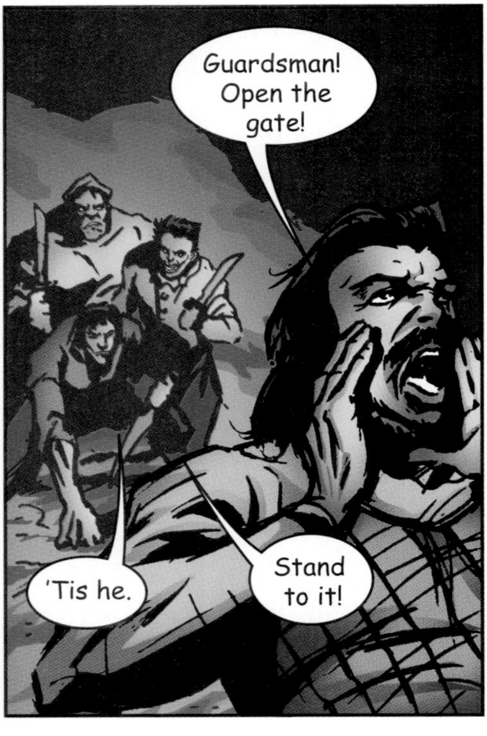
Guardsman! Open the gate!
'Tis he.
Stand to it!

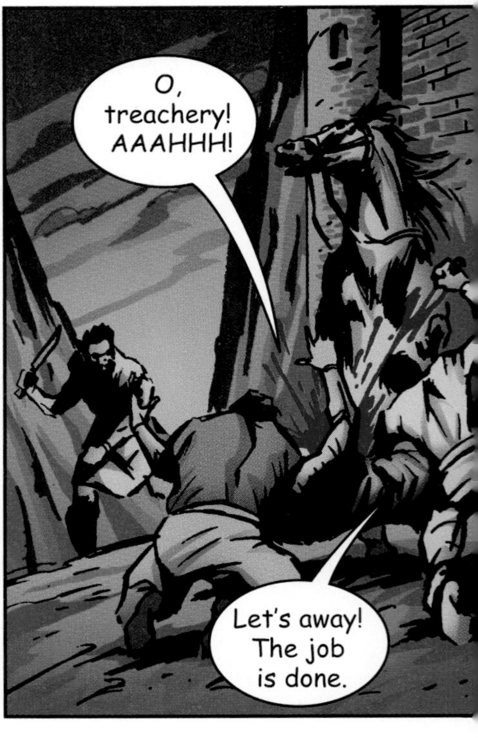
O, treachery! AAAHHH!
Let's away! The job is done.

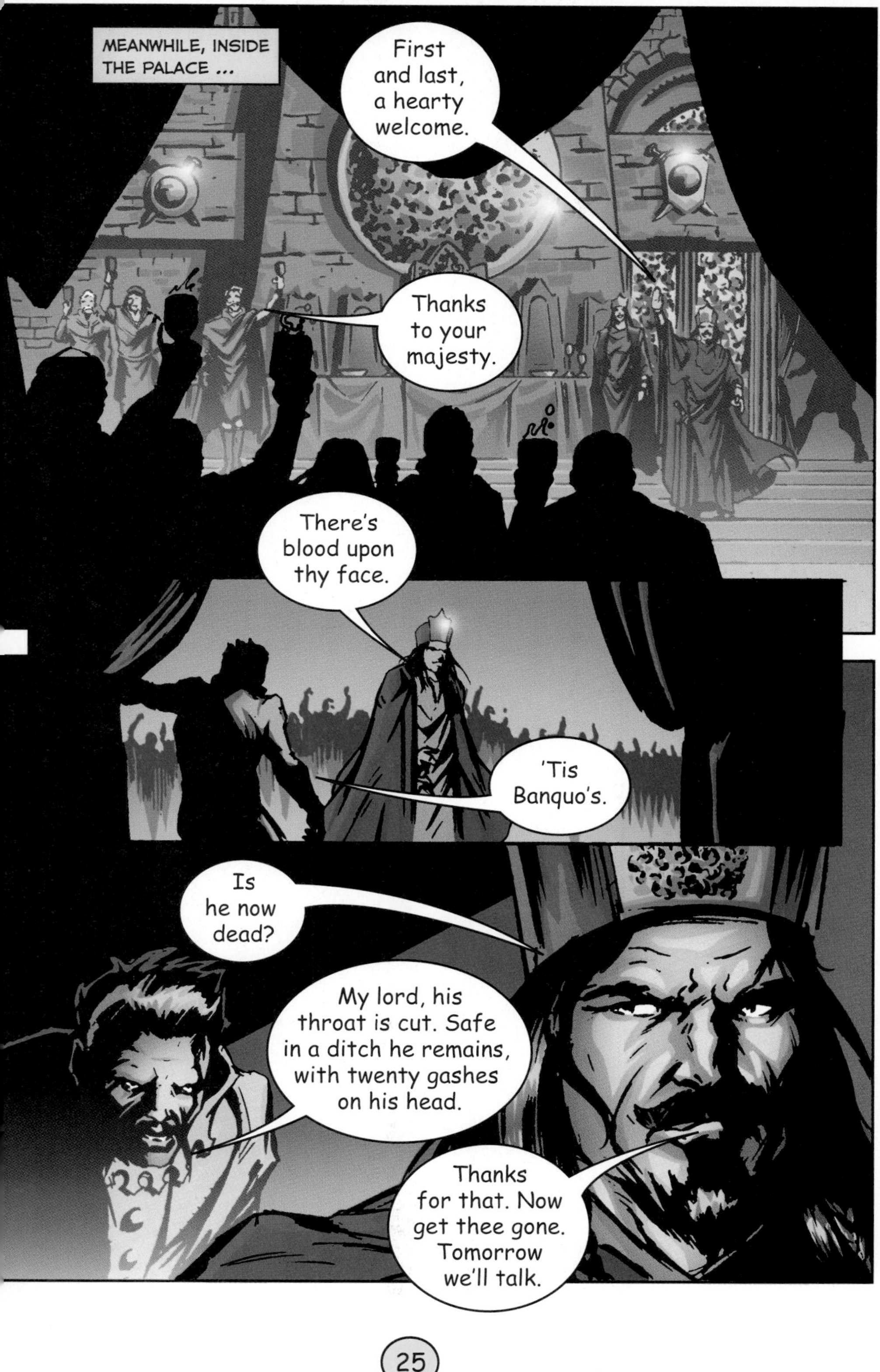
MEANWHILE, INSIDE THE PALACE ...
First and last, a hearty welcome.
Thanks to your majesty.
There's blood upon thy face.
'Tis Banquo's.
Is he now dead?
My lord, his throat is cut. Safe in a ditch he remains, with twenty gashes on his head.
Thanks for that. Now get thee gone. Tomorrow we'll talk.

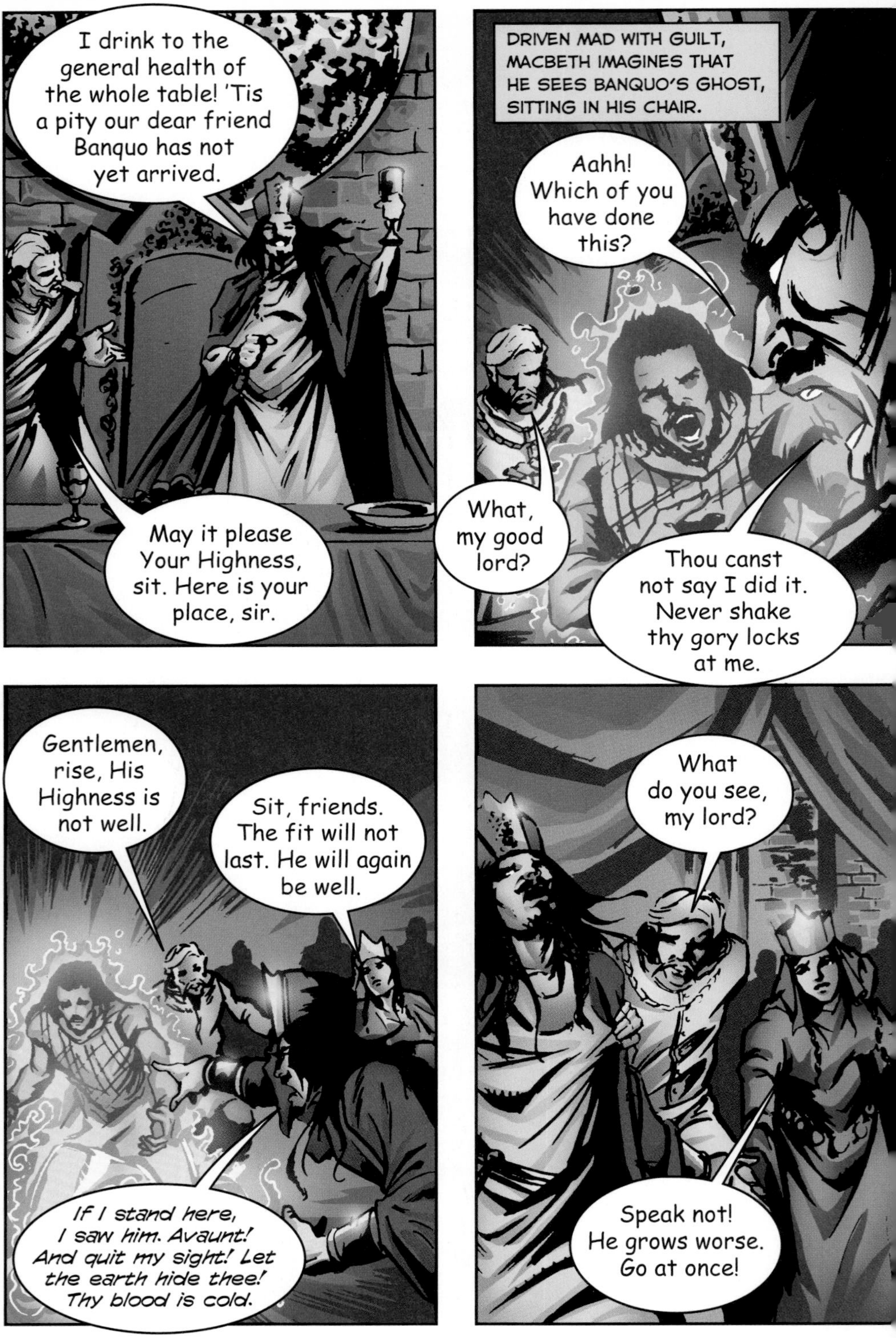
I drink to the general health of the whole table! 'Tis a pity our dear friend Banquo has not yet arrived.
May it please Your Highness, sit. Here is your place, sir.
DRIVEN MAD WITH GUILT, MACBETH IMAGINES THAT HE SEES BANQUO'S GHOST, SITTING IN HIS CHAIR.
Aahh! Which of you have done this?
What, my good lord?
Thou canst not say I did it. Never shake thy gory locks at me.
Gentlemen, rise, His Highness is not well.
Sit, friends. The fit will not last. He will again be well.
If I stand here, I saw him. Avaunt! And quit my sight! Let the earth hide thee! Thy blood is cold.
What do you see, my lord?
Speak not! He grows worse. Go at once!

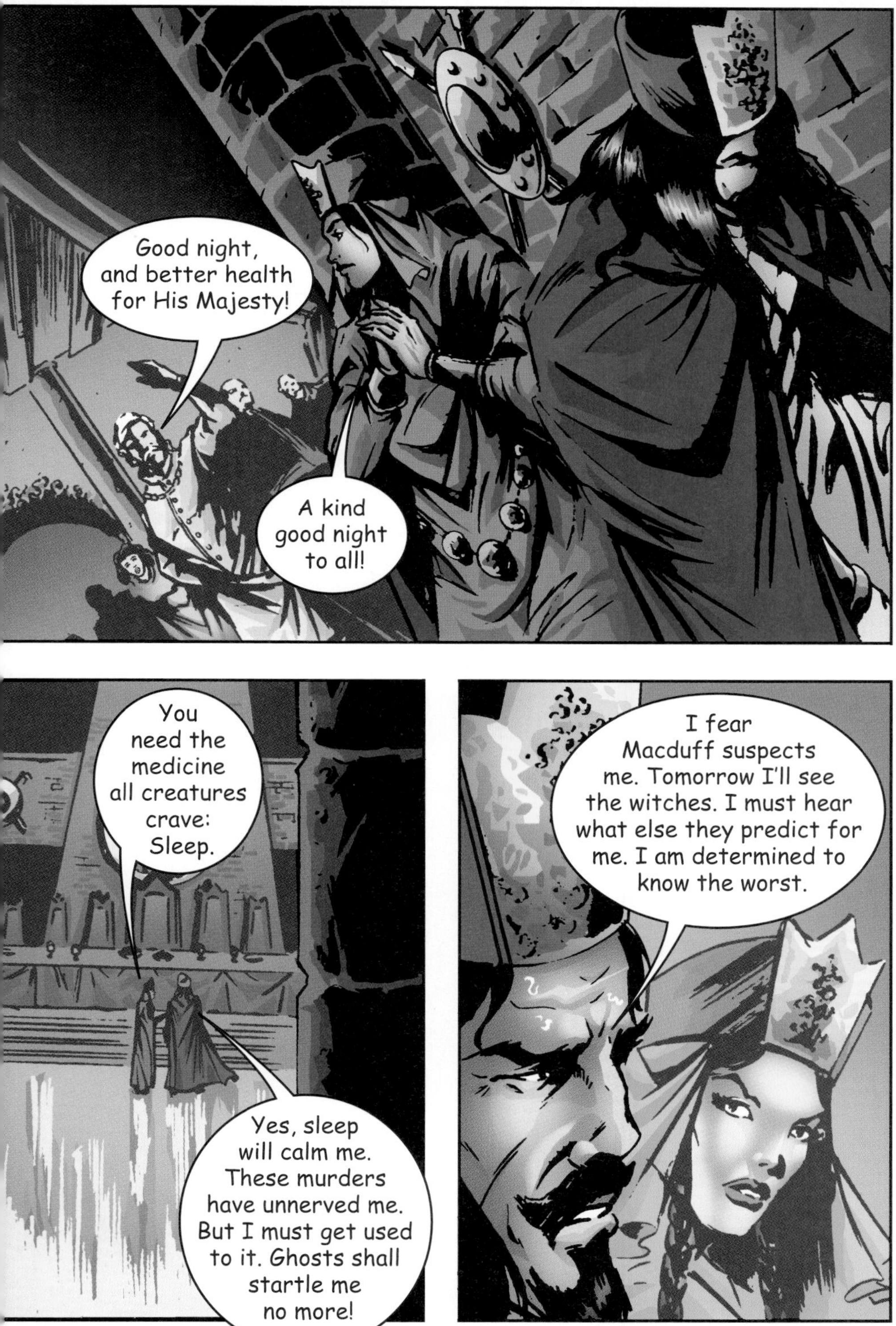
Good night, and better health for His Majesty!
A kind good night to all!
You need the medicine all creatures crave: Sleep.
Yes, sleep will calm me. These murders have unnerved me. But I must get used to it. Ghosts shall startle me no more!
I fear Macduff suspects me. Tomorrow I'll see the witches. I must hear what else they predict for me. I am determined to know the worst.

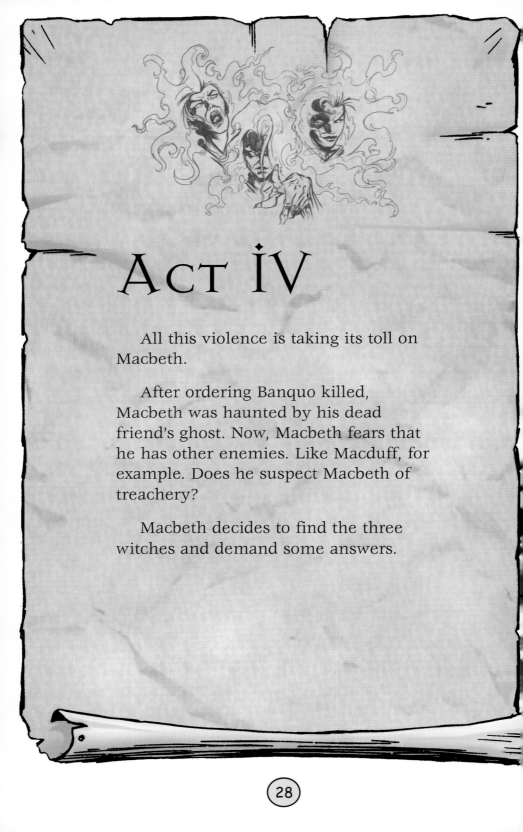

Act IV

All this violence is taking its toll on Macbeth.

After ordering Banquo killed, Macbeth was haunted by his dead friend's ghost. Now, Macbeth fears that he has other enemies. Like Macduff, for example. Does he suspect Macbeth of treachery?

Macbeth decides to find the three witches and demand some answers.

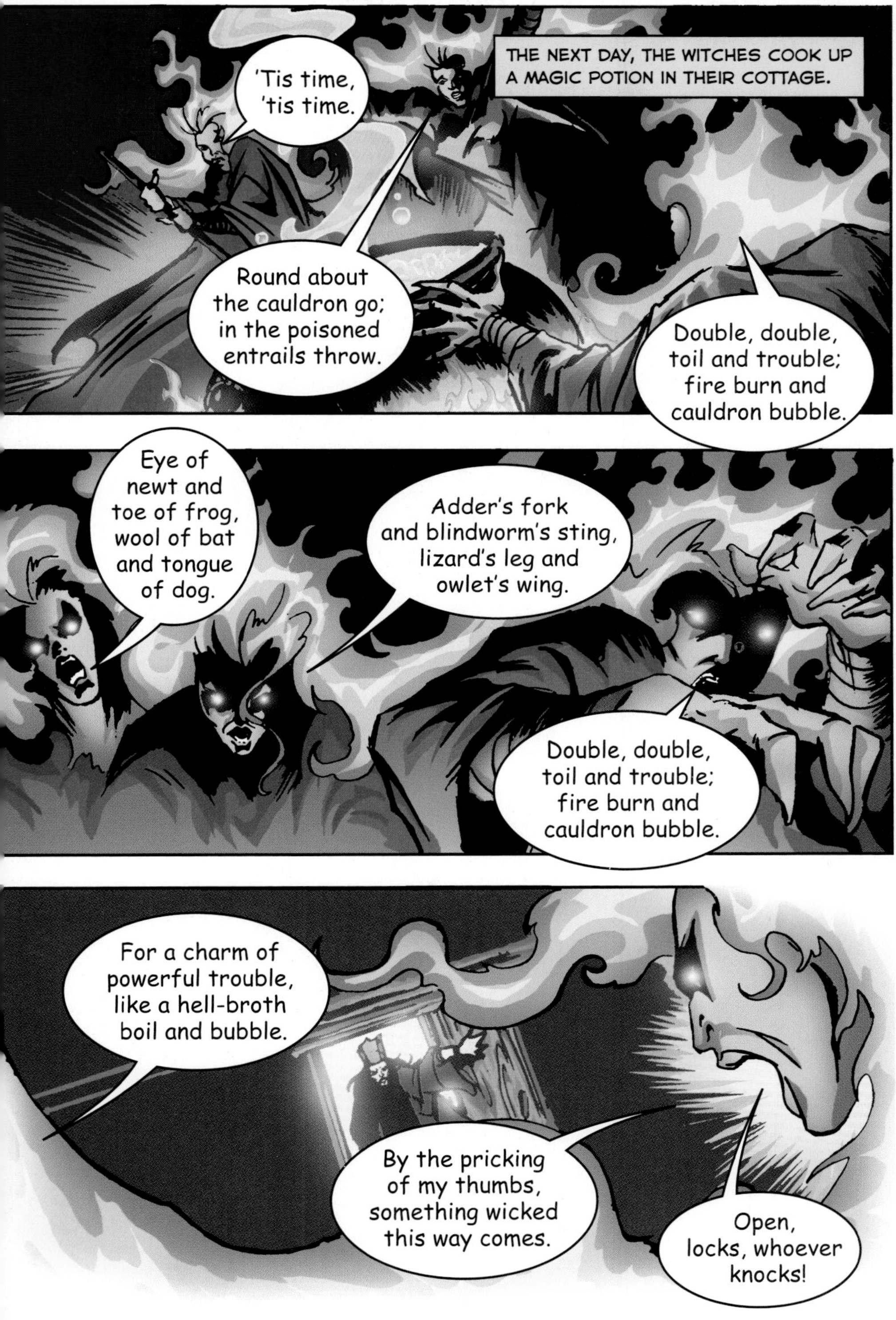
THE NEXT DAY, THE WITCHES COOK UP A MAGIC POTION IN THEIR COTTAGE.
'Tis time, 'tis time.
Round about the cauldron go; in the poisoned entrails throw.
Double, double, toil and trouble; fire burn and cauldron bubble.
Eye of newt and toe of frog, wool of bat and tongue of dog.
Adder's fork and blindworm's sting, lizard's leg and owlet's wing.
Double, double, toil and trouble; fire burn and cauldron bubble.
For a charm of powerful trouble, like a hell-broth boil and bubble.
By the pricking of my thumbs, something wicked this way comes.
Open, locks, whoever knocks!

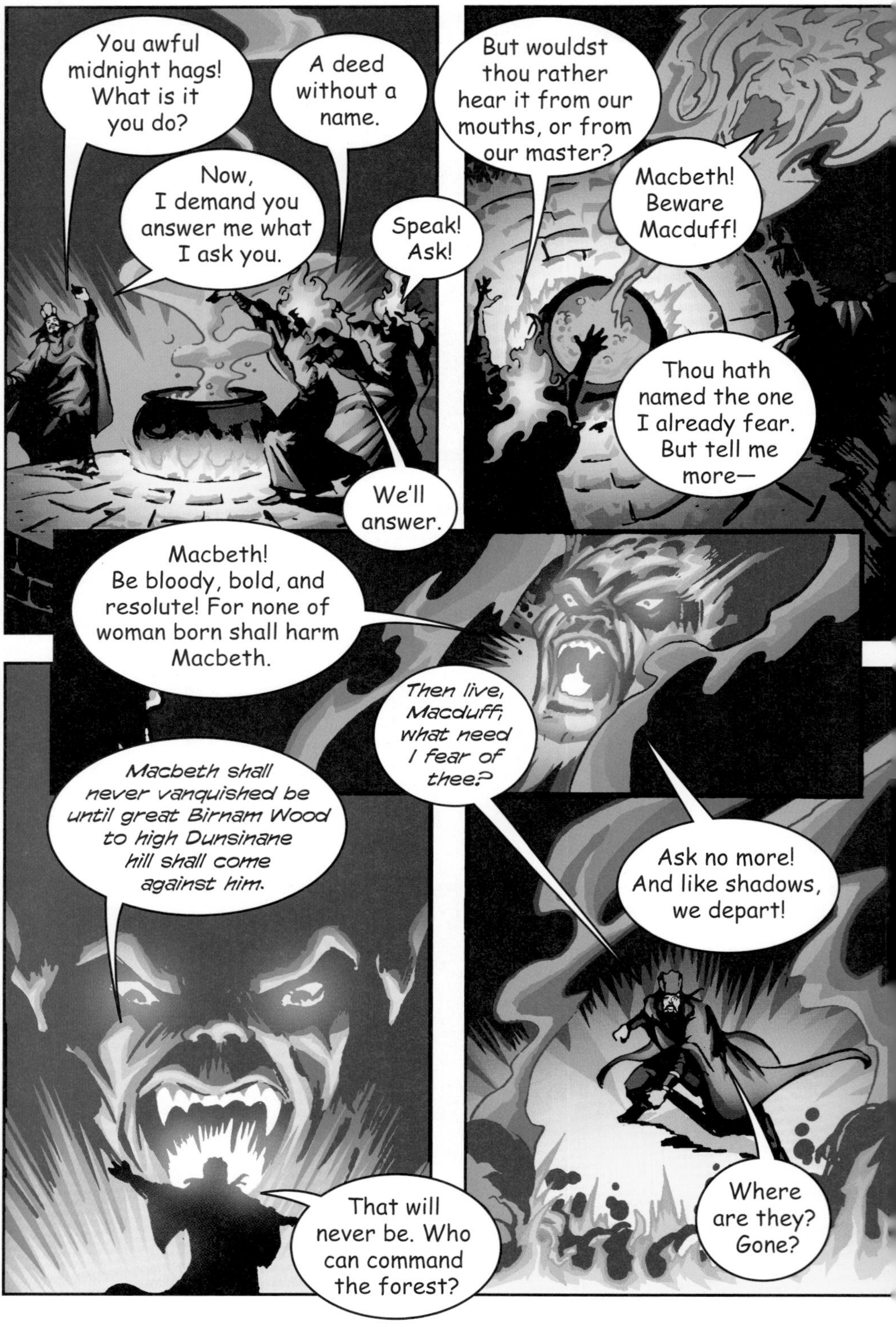
You awful midnight hags! What is it you do?
A deed without a name.
Now, I demand you answer me what I ask you.
Speak! Ask!
We'll answer.
But wouldst thou rather hear it from our mouths, or from our master?
Macbeth! Beware Macduff!
Thou hath named the one I already fear. But tell me more—
Macbeth! Be bloody, bold, and resolute! For none of woman born shall harm Macbeth.
Then live, Macduff; what need I fear of thee?
Macbeth shall never vanquished be until great Birnam Wood to high Dunsinane hill shall come against him.
That will never be. Who can command the forest?
Ask no more! And like shadows, we depart!
Where are they? Gone?

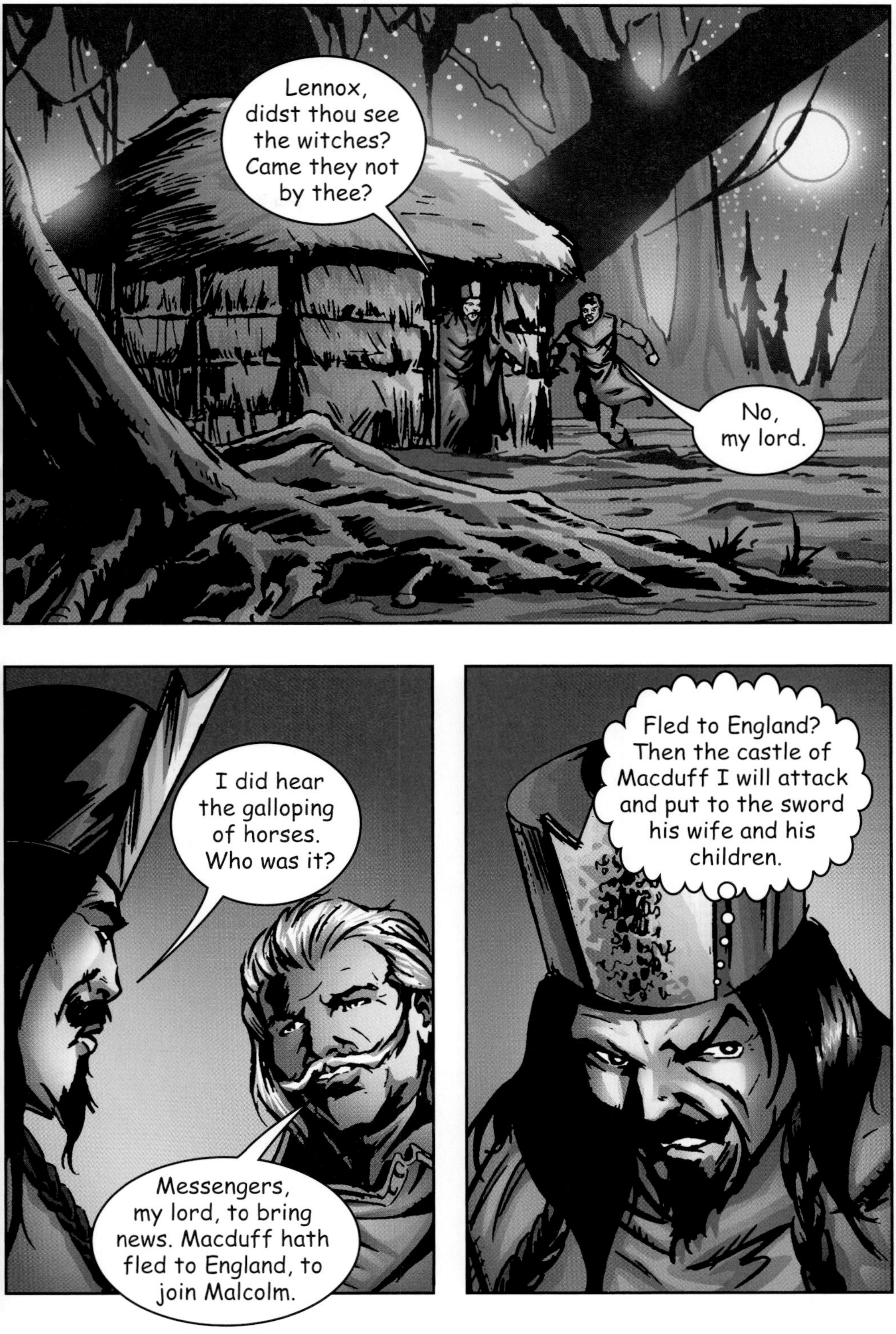
Lennox, didst thou see the witches? Came they not by thee?
No, my lord.
I did hear the galloping of horses. Who was it?
Messengers, my lord, to bring news. Macduff hath fled to England, to join Malcolm.
Fled to England? Then the castle of Macduff I will attack and put to the sword his wife and his children.

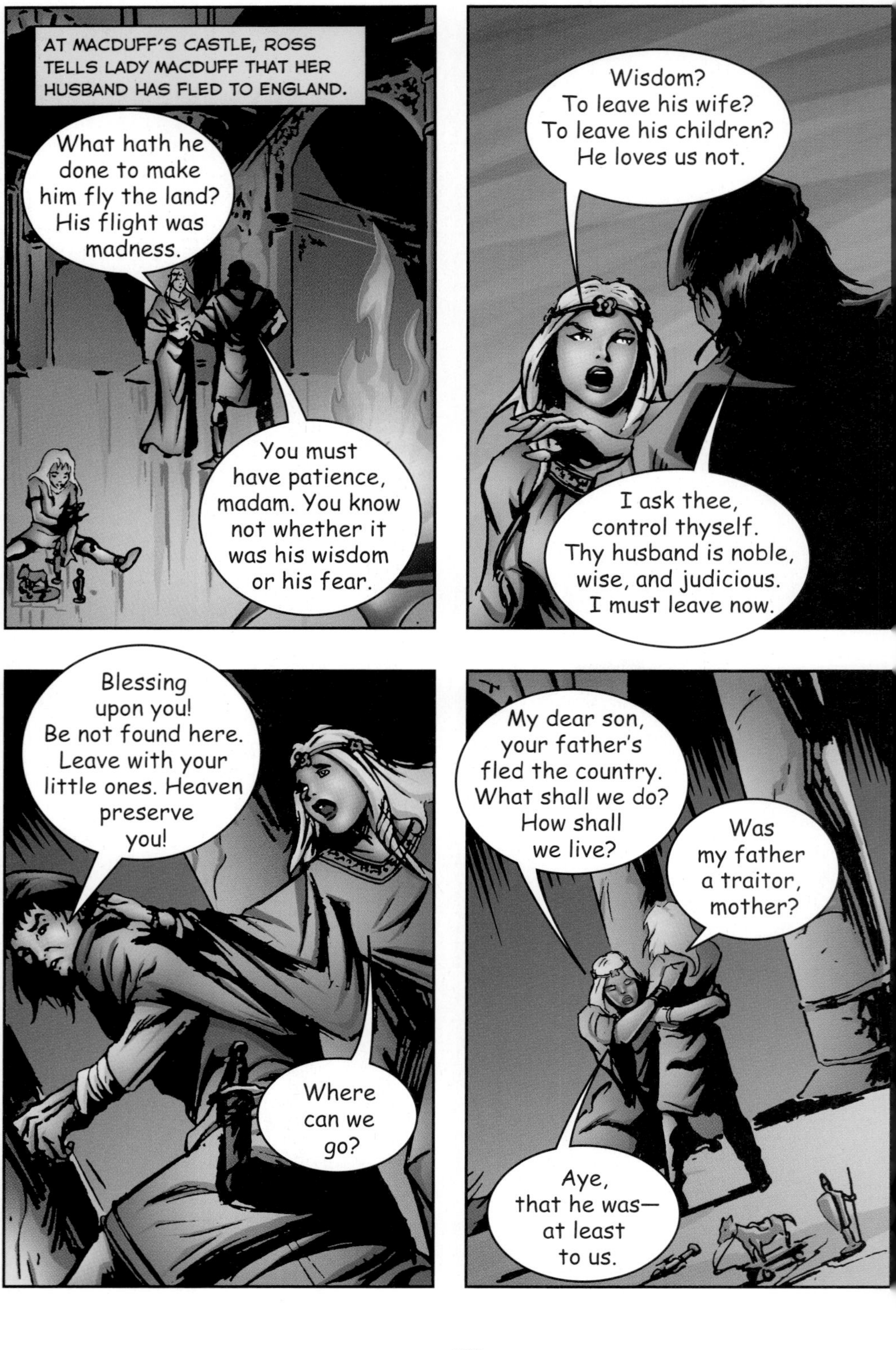
AT MACDUFF'S CASTLE, ROSS TELLS LADY MACDUFF THAT HER HUSBAND HAS FLED TO ENGLAND.
What hath he done to make him fly the land? His flight was madness.
You must have patience, madam. You know not whether it was his wisdom or his fear.
Wisdom? To leave his wife? To leave his children? He loves us not.
I ask thee, control thyself. Thy husband is noble, wise, and judicious. I must leave now.
Blessing upon you! Be not found here. Leave with your little ones. Heaven preserve you!
Where can we go?
My dear son, your father's fled the country. What shall we do? How shall we live?
Was my father a traitor, mother?
Aye, that he was— at least to us.

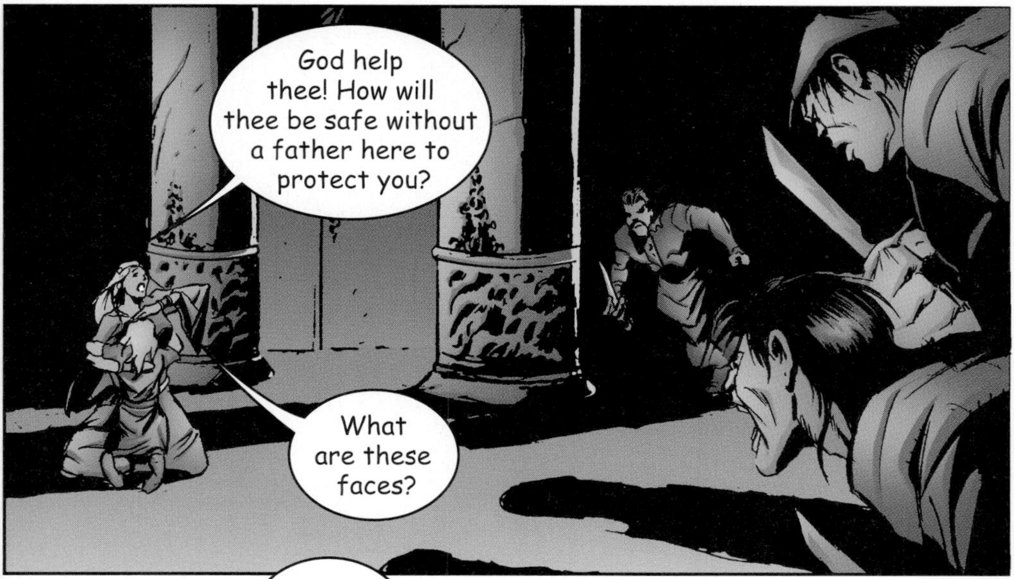
God help thee! How will thee be safe without a father here to protect you?
What are these faces?

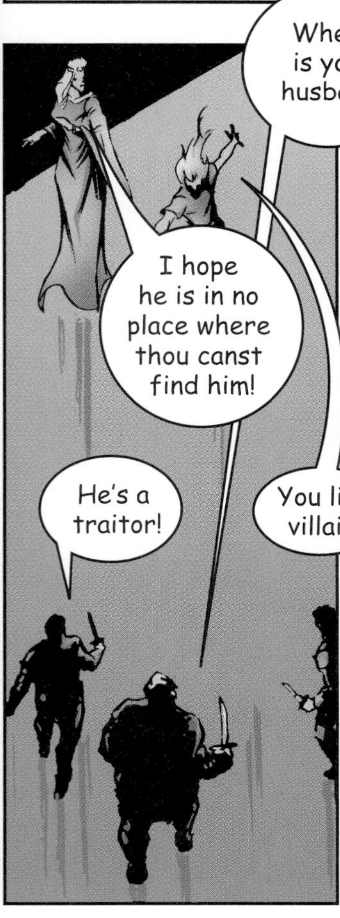
Where is your husband?
I hope he is in no place where thou canst find him!
He's a traitor!
You lie, villain!

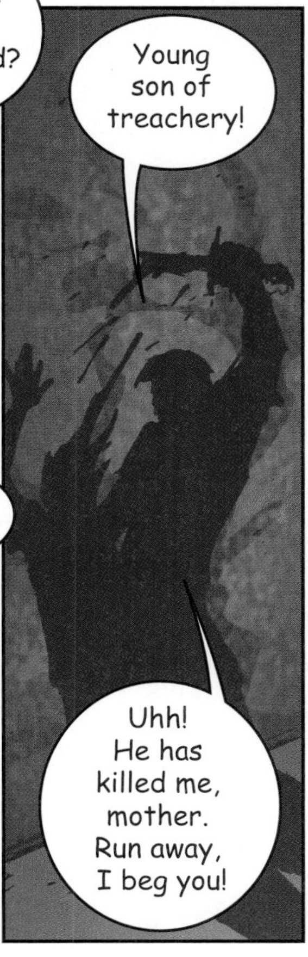
Young son of treachery!
Uhh! He has killed me, mother. Run away, I beg you!

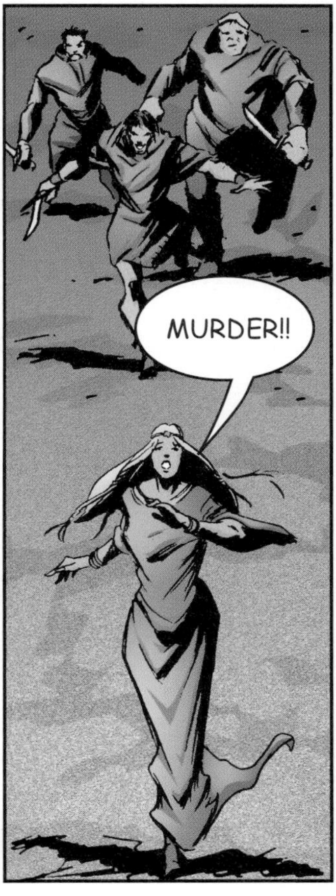
MURDER!!

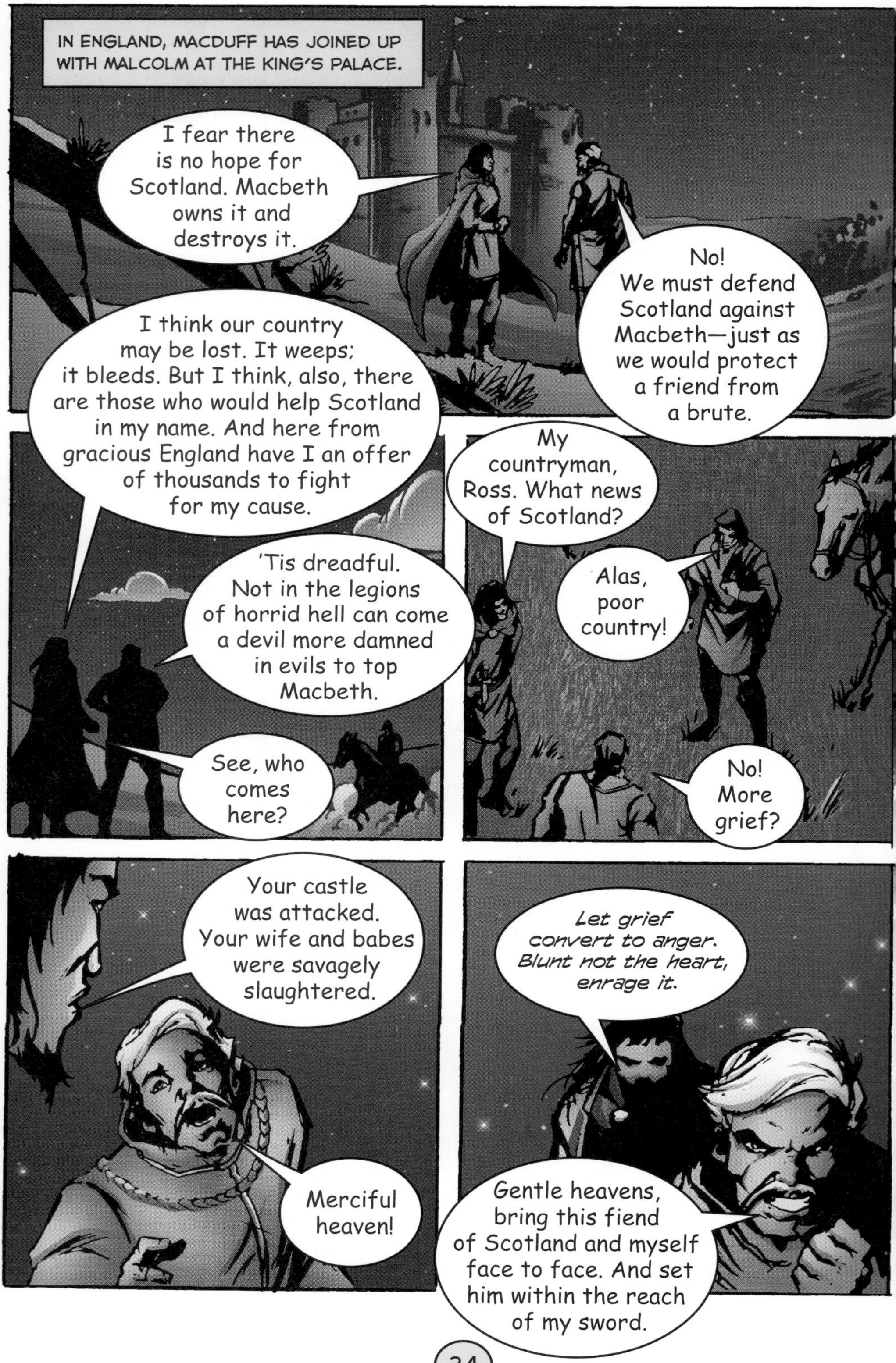
IN ENGLAND, MACDUFF HAS JOINED UP WITH MALCOLM AT THE KING'S PALACE.
I fear there is no hope for Scotland. Macbeth owns it and destroys it.
No! We must defend Scotland against Macbeth—just as we would protect a friend from a brute.
I think our country may be lost. It weeps; it bleeds. But I think, also, there are those who would help Scotland in my name. And here from gracious England have I an offer of thousands to fight for my cause.
'Tis dreadful. Not in the legions of horrid hell can come a devil more damned in evils to top Macbeth.
See, who comes here?
My countryman, Ross. What news of Scotland?
Alas, poor country!
No! More grief?
Your castle was attacked. Your wife and babes were savagely slaughtered.
Merciful heaven!
Let grief convert to anger. Blunt not the heart, enrage it.
Gentle heavens, bring this fiend of Scotland and myself face to face. And set him within the reach of my sword.

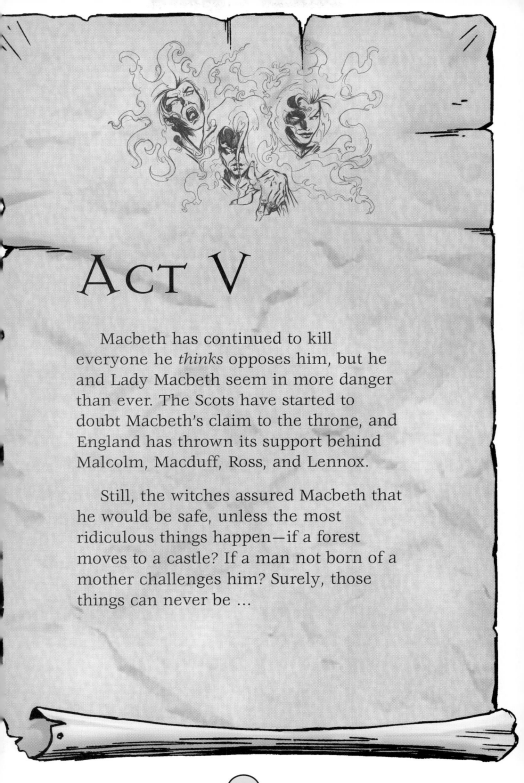

Act V

Macbeth has continued to kill everyone he *thinks* opposes him, but he and Lady Macbeth seem in more danger than ever. The Scots have started to doubt Macbeth's claim to the throne, and England has thrown its support behind Malcolm, Macduff, Ross, and Lennox.

Still, the witches assured Macbeth that he would be safe, unless the most ridiculous things happen—if a forest moves to a castle? If a man not born of a mother challenges him? Surely, those things can never be ...

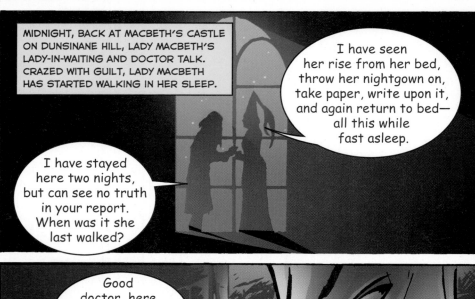

MIDNIGHT, BACK AT MACBETH'S CASTLE ON DUNSINANE HILL, LADY MACBETH'S LADY-IN-WAITING AND DOCTOR TALK. CRAZED WITH GUILT, LADY MACBETH HAS STARTED WALKING IN HER SLEEP.

I have seen her rise from her bed, throw her nightgown on, take paper, write upon it, and again return to bed— all this while fast asleep.

I have stayed here two nights, but can see no truth in your report. When was it she last walked?

Good doctor, here she comes! And upon my life, fast asleep!

No. She is awake. See, her eyes are open.

Yes, but her mind is closed.

Yet here's a spot.

36

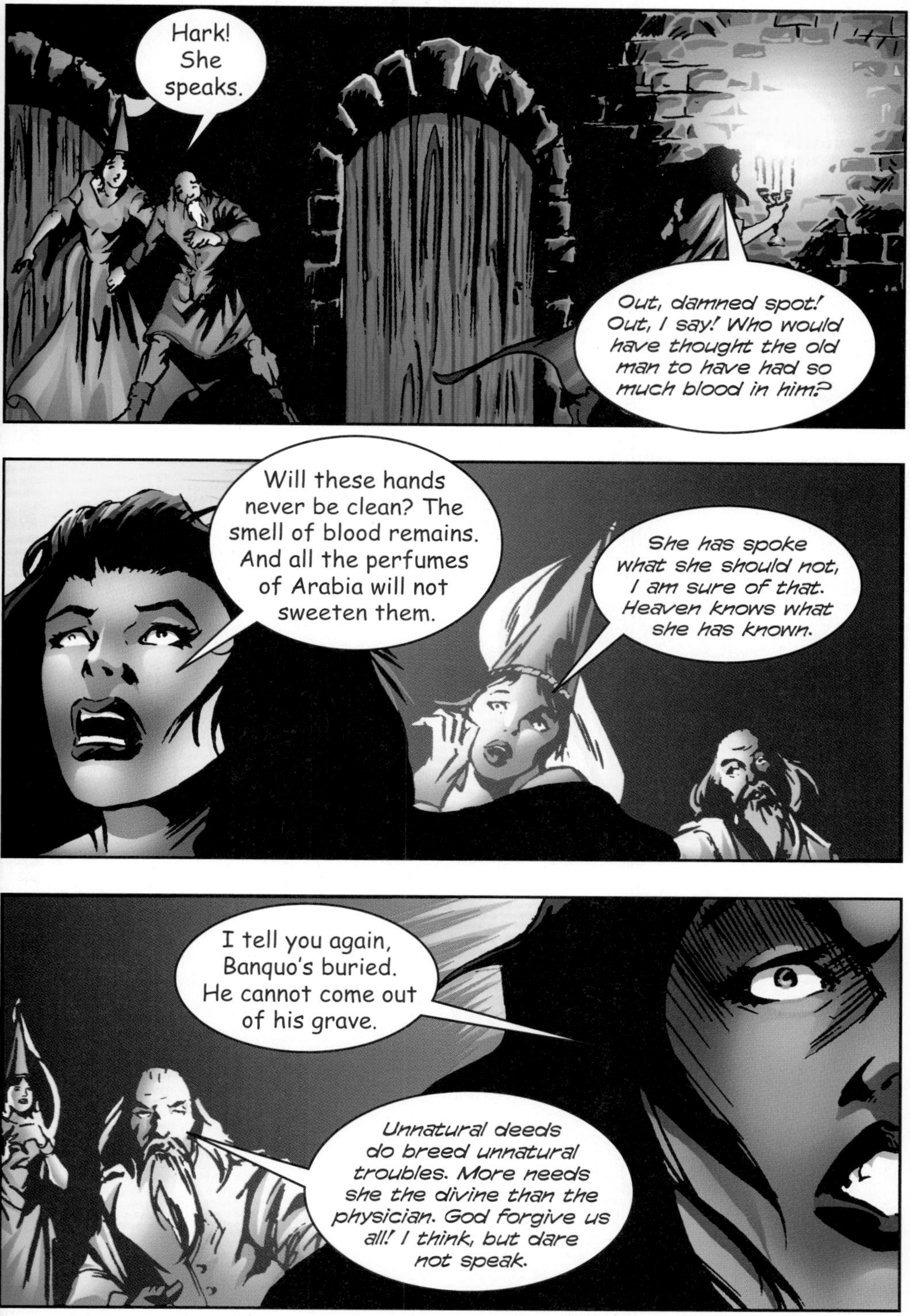
Hark! She speaks.
Out, damned spot! Out, I say! Who would have thought the old man to have had so much blood in him?
Will these hands never be clean? The smell of blood remains. And all the perfumes of Arabia will not sweeten them.
She has spoke what she should not, I am sure of that. Heaven knows what she has known.
I tell you again, Banquo's buried. He cannot come out of his grave.
Unnatural deeds do breed unnatural troubles. More needs she the divine than the physician. God forgive us all! I think, but dare not speak.

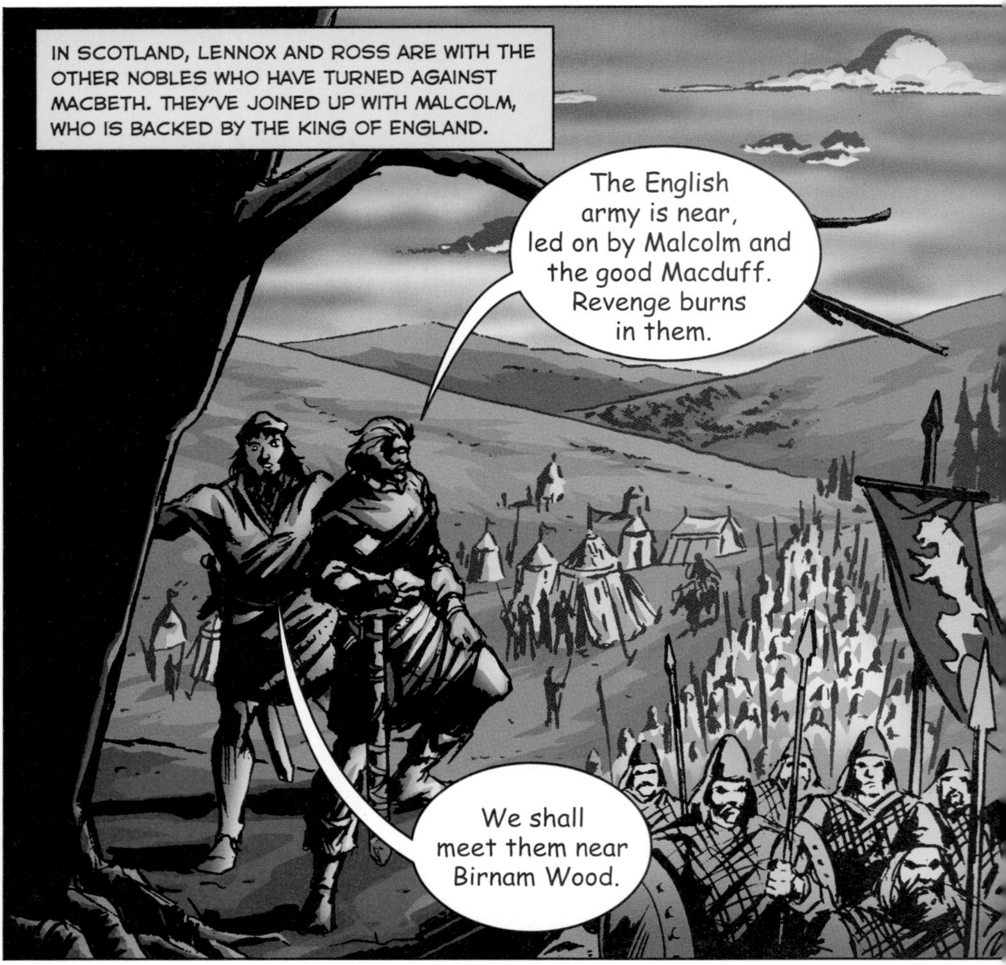
IN SCOTLAND, LENNOX AND ROSS ARE WITH THE OTHER NOBLES WHO HAVE TURNED AGAINST MACBETH. THEY'VE JOINED UP WITH MALCOLM, WHO IS BACKED BY THE KING OF ENGLAND.
The English army is near, led on by Malcolm and the good Macduff. Revenge burns in them.
We shall meet them near Birnam Wood.

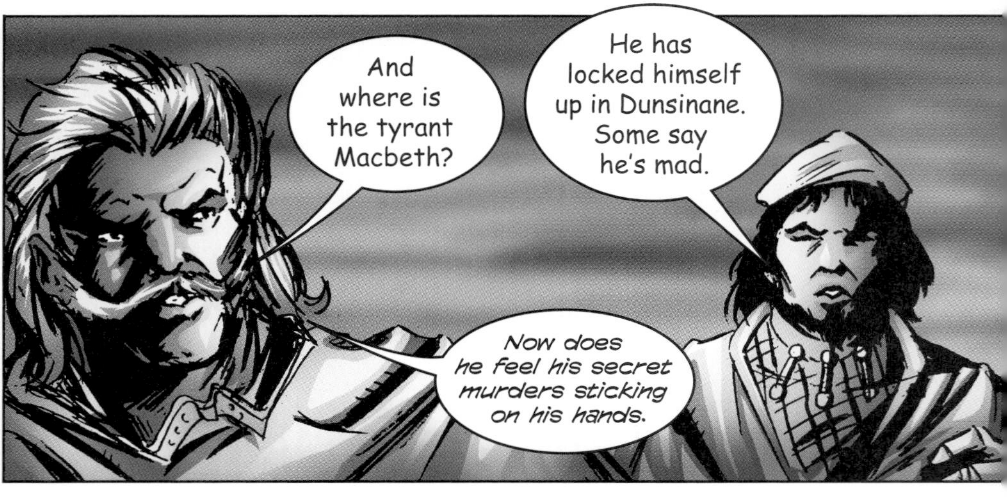
And where is the tyrant Macbeth?
He has locked himself up in Dunsinane. Some say he's mad.
Now does he feel his secret murders sticking on his hands.

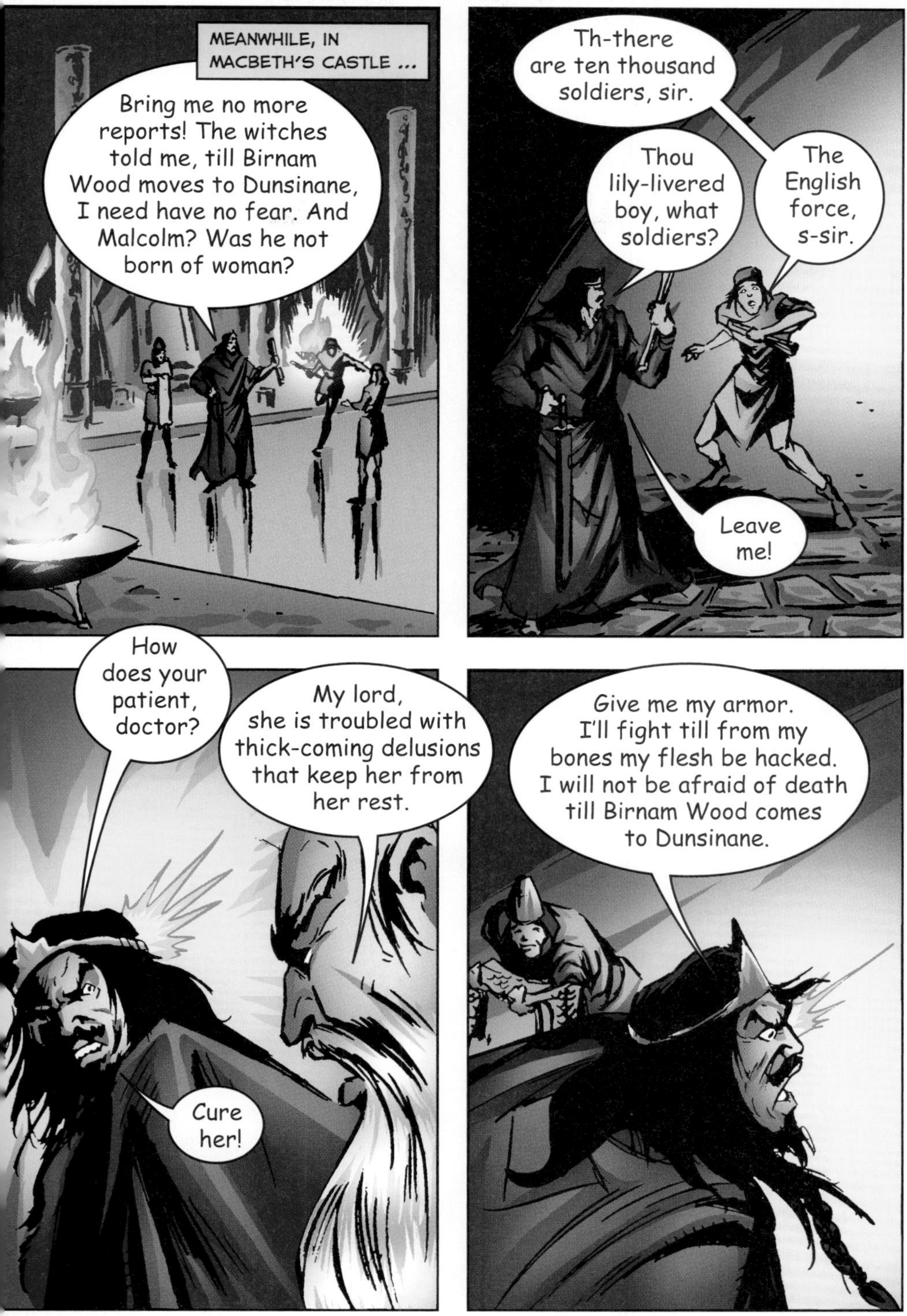
MEANWHILE, IN MACBETH'S CASTLE ...
Bring me no more reports! The witches told me, till Birnam Wood moves to Dunsinane, I need have no fear. And Malcolm? Was he not born of woman?
Th-there are ten thousand soldiers, sir.
Thou lily-livered boy, what soldiers?
The English force, s-sir.
Leave me!
How does your patient, doctor?
My lord, she is troubled with thick-coming delusions that keep her from her rest.
Cure her!
Give me my armor. I'll fight till from my bones my flesh be hacked. I will not be afraid of death till Birnam Wood comes to Dunsinane.

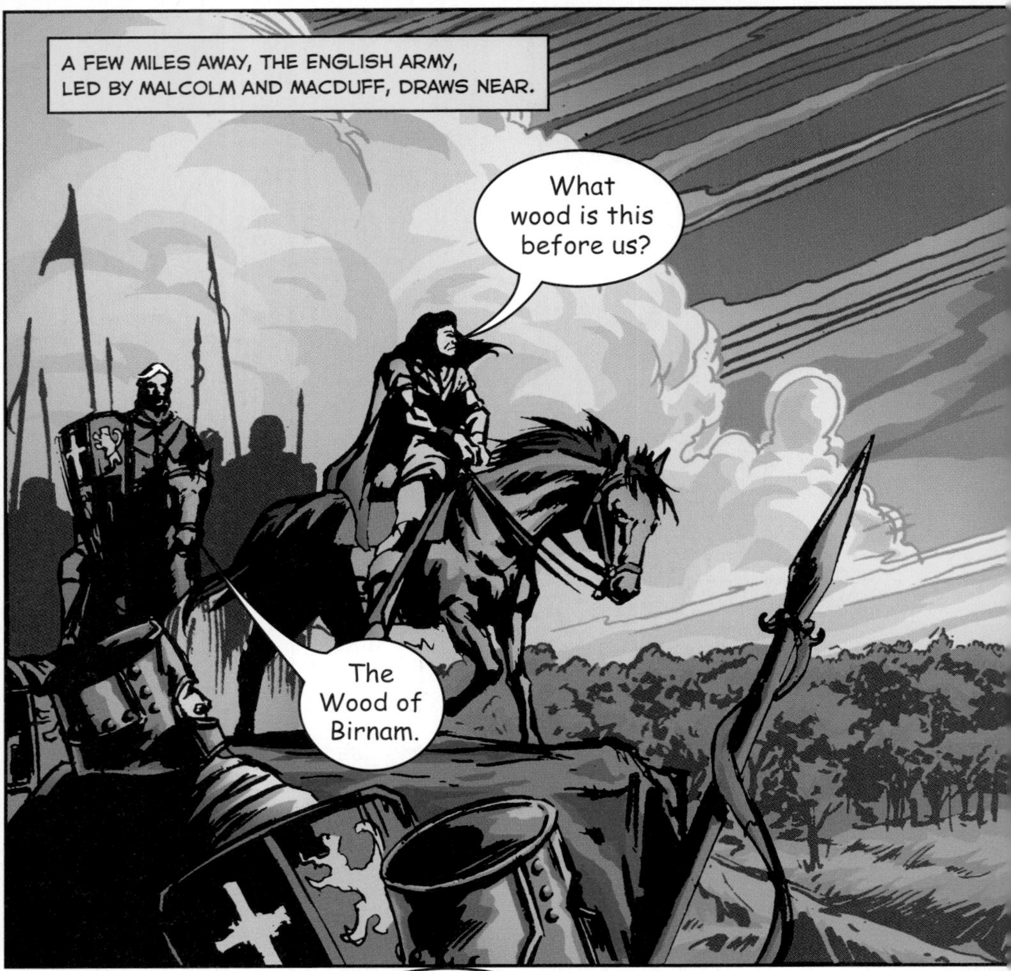
A FEW MILES AWAY, THE ENGLISH ARMY, LED BY MALCOLM AND MACDUFF, DRAWS NEAR.
What wood is this before us?
The Wood of Birnam.

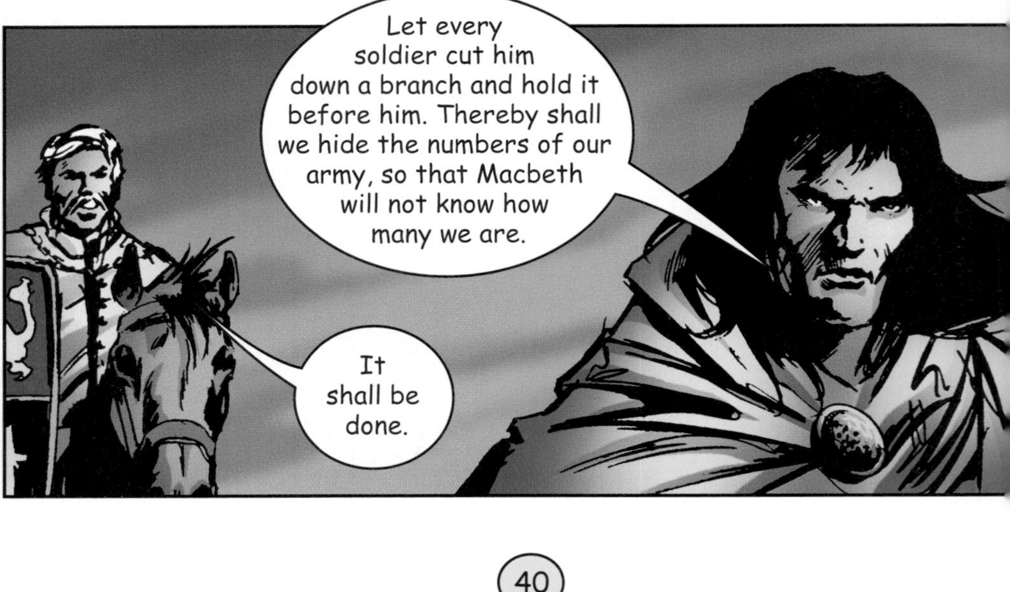
Let every soldier cut him down a branch and hold it before him. Thereby shall we hide the numbers of our army, so that Macbeth will not know how many we are.
It shall be done.

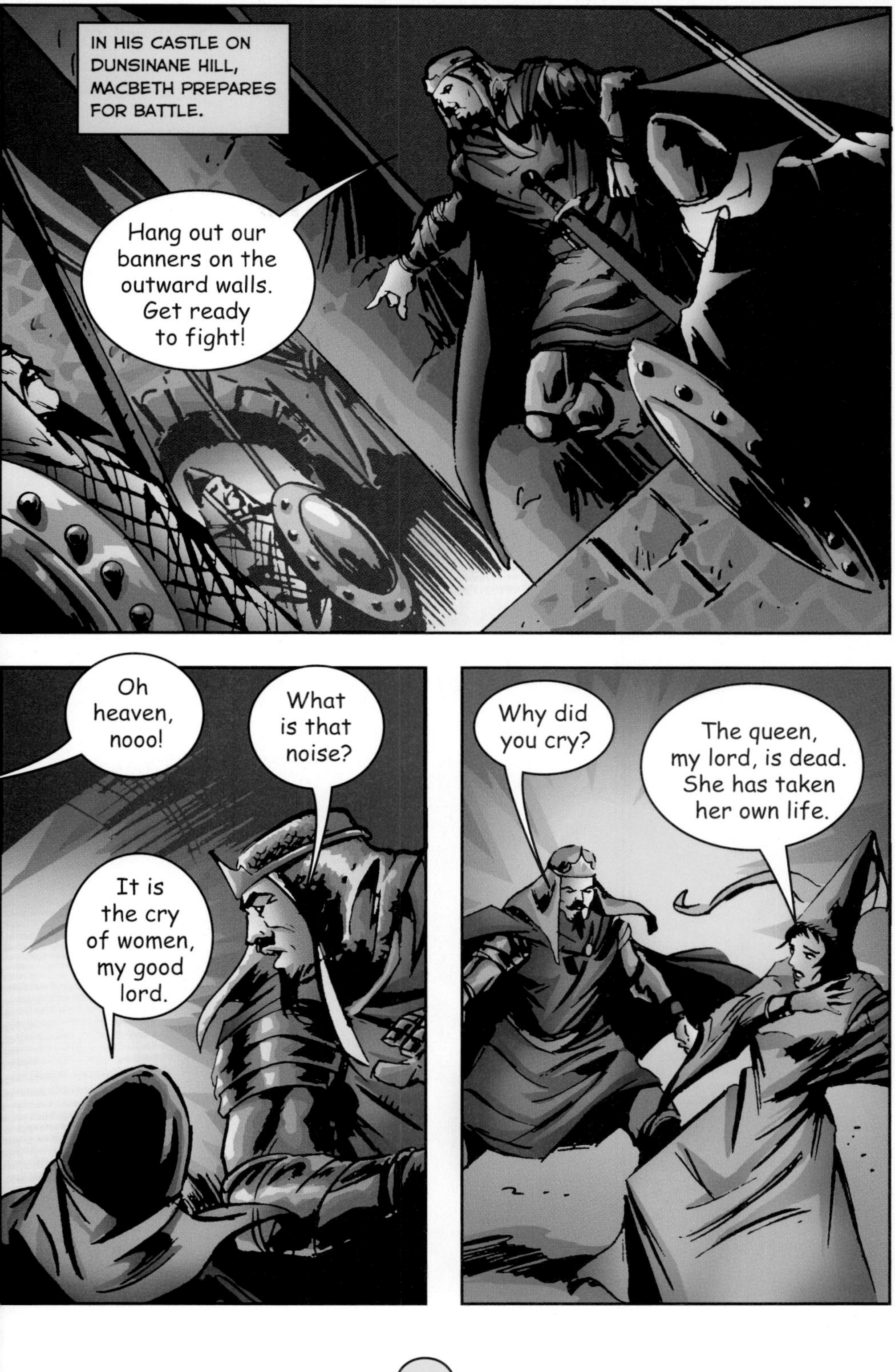
IN HIS CASTLE ON DUNSINANE HILL, MACBETH PREPARES FOR BATTLE.
Hang out our banners on the outward walls. Get ready to fight!
Oh heaven, nooo!
What is that noise?
It is the cry of women, my good lord.
Why did you cry?
The queen, my lord, is dead. She has taken her own life.

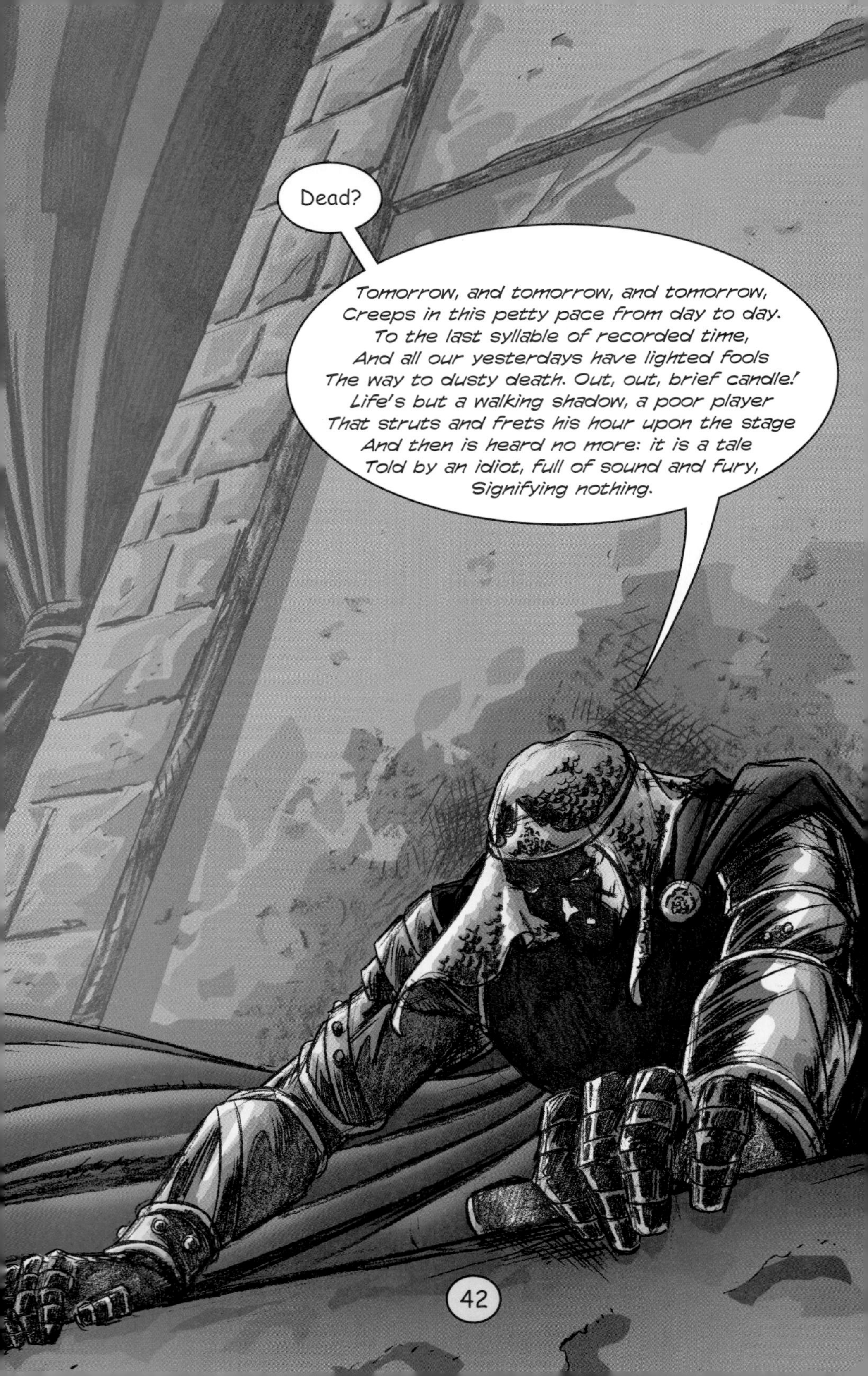
Dead?
Tomorrow, and tomorrow, and tomorrow, Creeps in this petty pace from day to day. To the last syllable of recorded time, And all our yesterdays have lighted fools The way to dusty death. Out, out, brief candle! Life's but a walking shadow, a poor player That struts and frets his hour upon the stage And then is heard no more: it is a tale Told by an idiot, full of sound and fury, Signifying nothing.

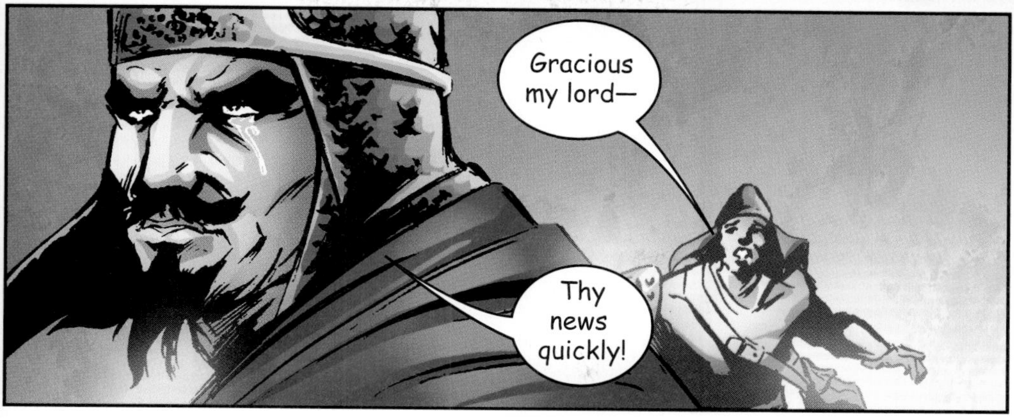
Gracious my lord—
Thy news quickly!

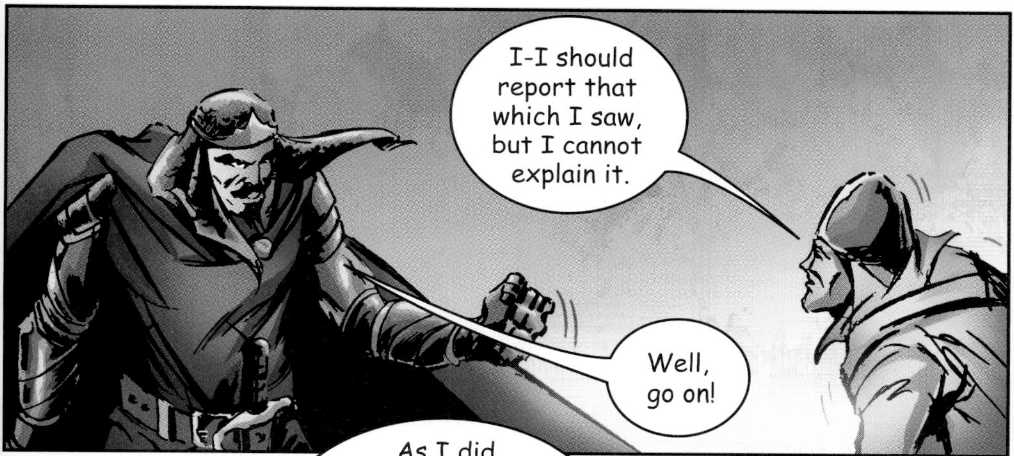
I-I should report that which I saw, but I cannot explain it.
Well, go on!

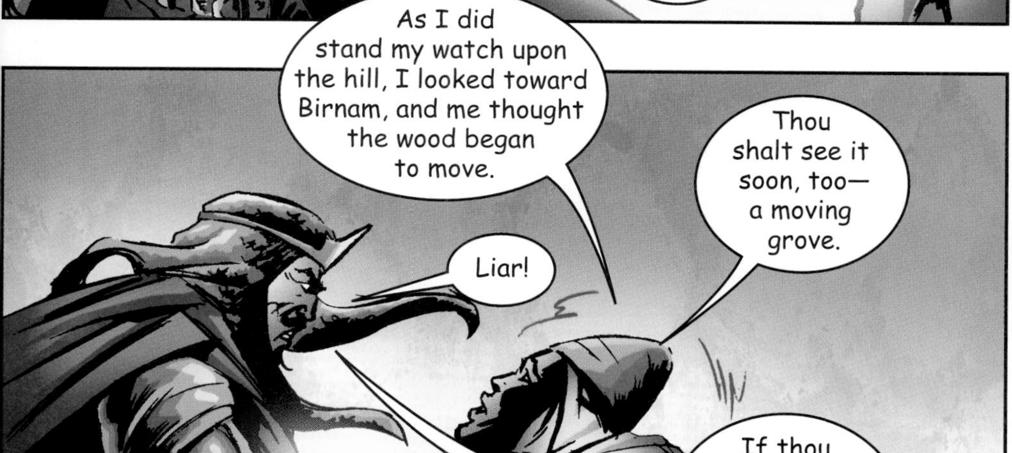
As I did stand my watch upon the hill, I looked toward Birnam, and me thought the wood began to move.
Liar!
Thou shalt see it soon, too— a moving grove.
If thou speak false, upon the next tree thou shalt hang.

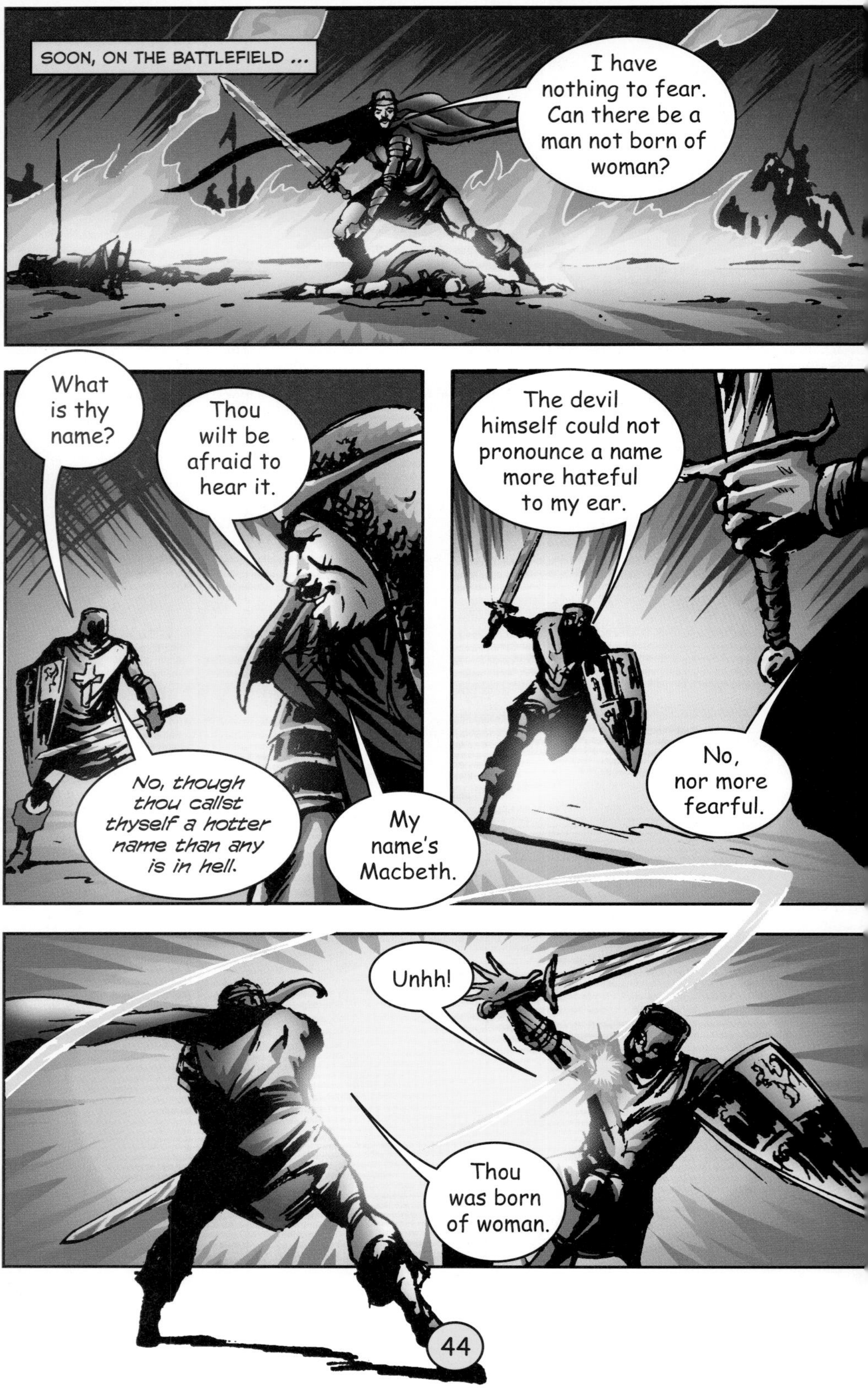

SOON, ON THE BATTLEFIELD ...
I have nothing to fear. Can there be a man not born of woman?
What is thy name?
Thou wilt be afraid to hear it.
No, though thou callst thyself a hotter name than any is in hell.
My name's Macbeth.
The devil himself could not pronounce a name more hateful to my ear.
No, nor more fearful.
Unhh!
Thou was born of woman.

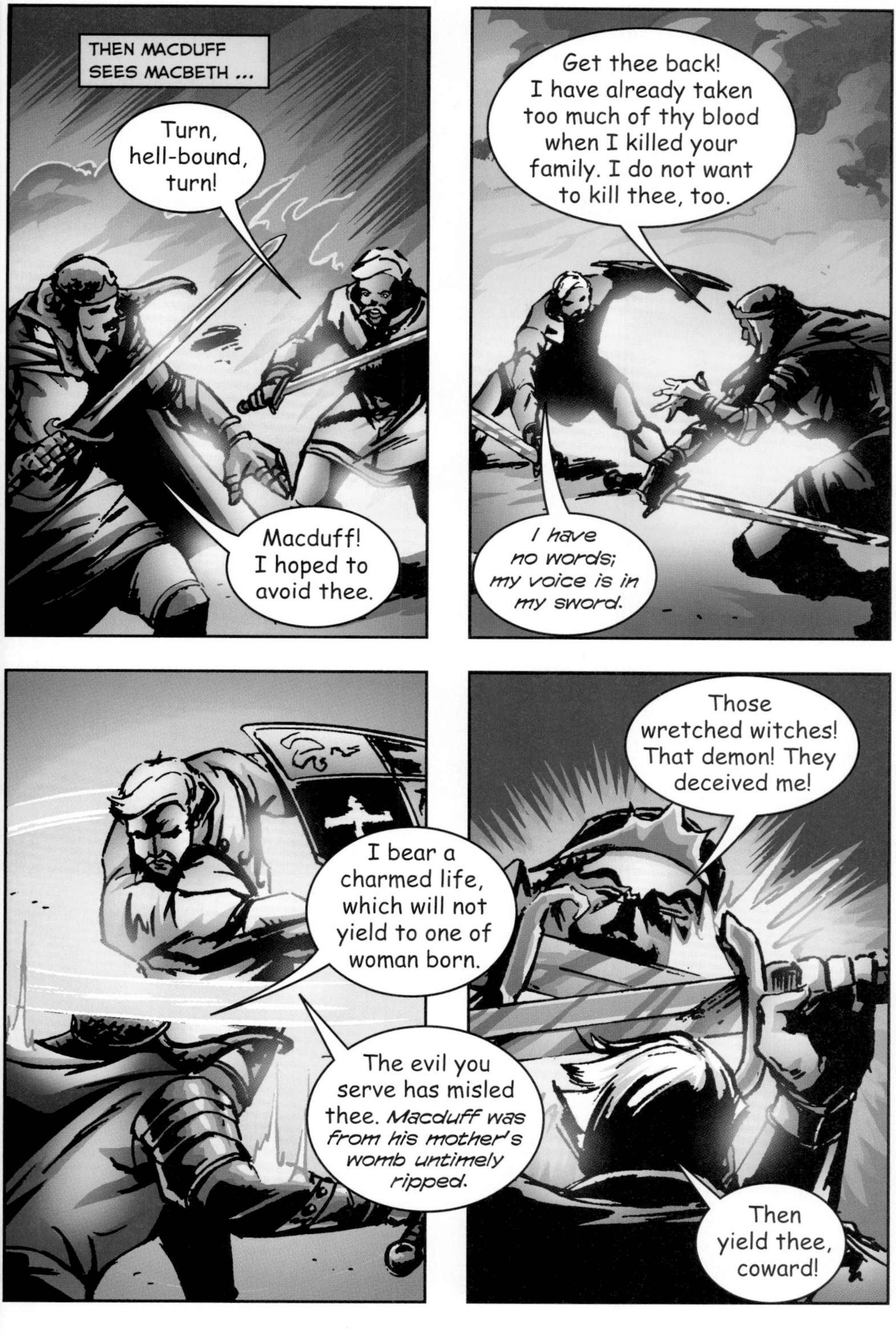
THEN MACDUFF SEES MACBETH ...
Turn, hell-bound, turn!
Macduff! I hoped to avoid thee.
Get thee back! I have already taken too much of thy blood when I killed your family. I do not want to kill thee, too.
I have no words; my voice is in my sword.
I bear a charmed life, which will not yield to one of woman born.
The evil you serve has misled thee. *Macduff was from his mother's womb untimely ripped.*
Those wretched witches! That demon! They deceived me!
Then yield thee, coward!

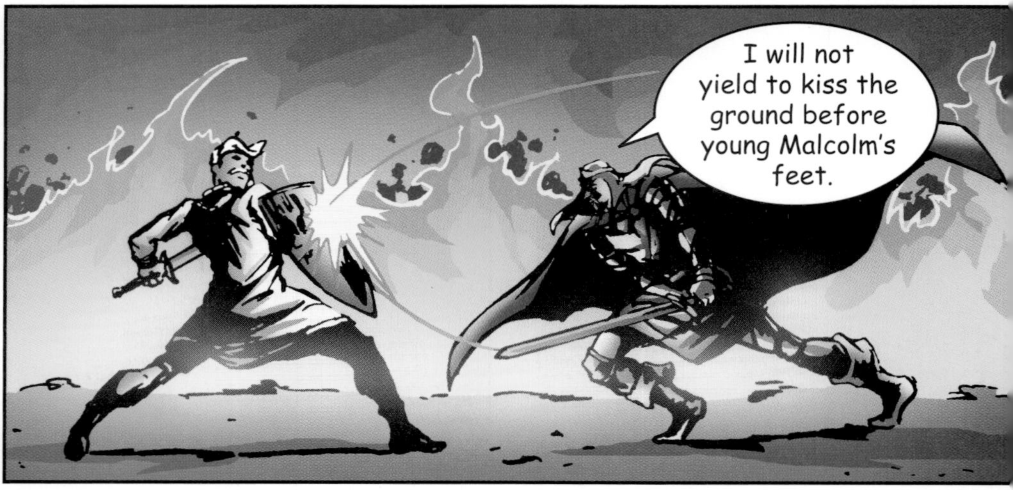
I will not yield to kiss the ground before young Malcolm's feet.

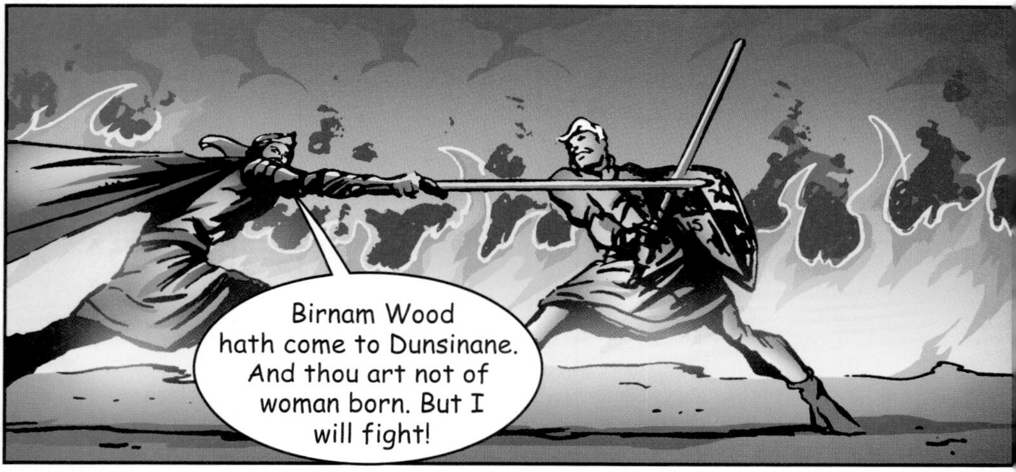
Birnam Wood hath come to Dunsinane. And thou art not of woman born. But I will fight!

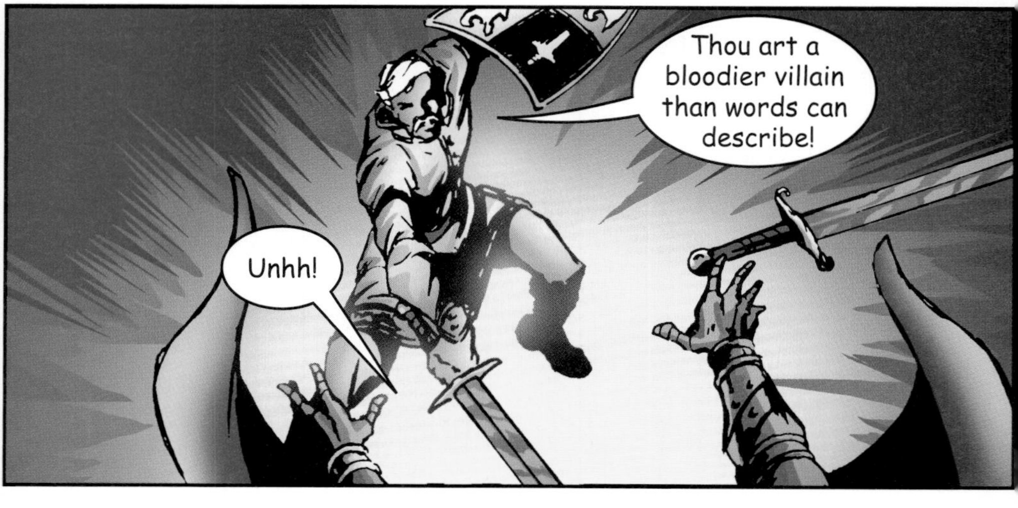
Thou art a bloodier villain than words can describe!
Unhh!

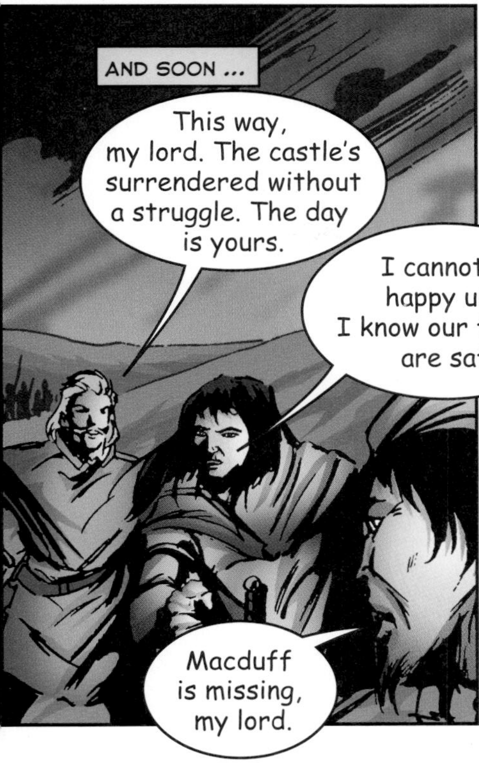
AND SOON ...
This way, my lord. The castle's surrendered without a struggle. The day is yours.
I cannot be happy until I know our friends are safe.
Macduff is missing, my lord.

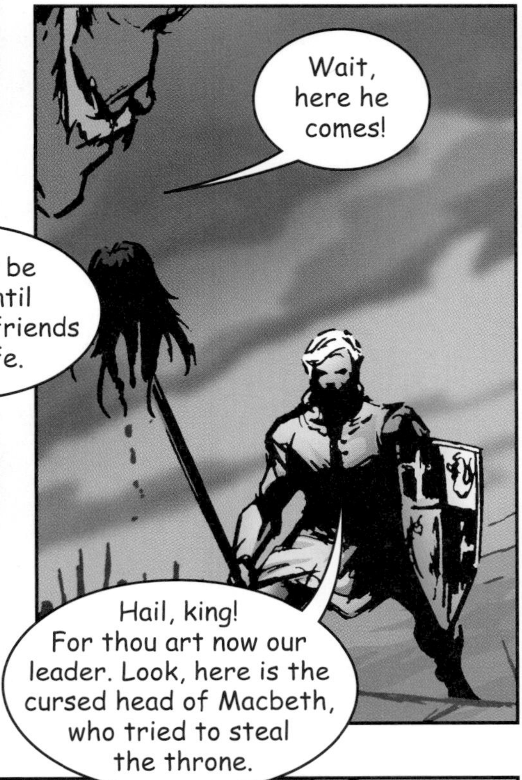
Wait, here he comes!
Hail, king! For thou art now our leader. Look, here is the cursed head of Macbeth, who tried to steal the throne.

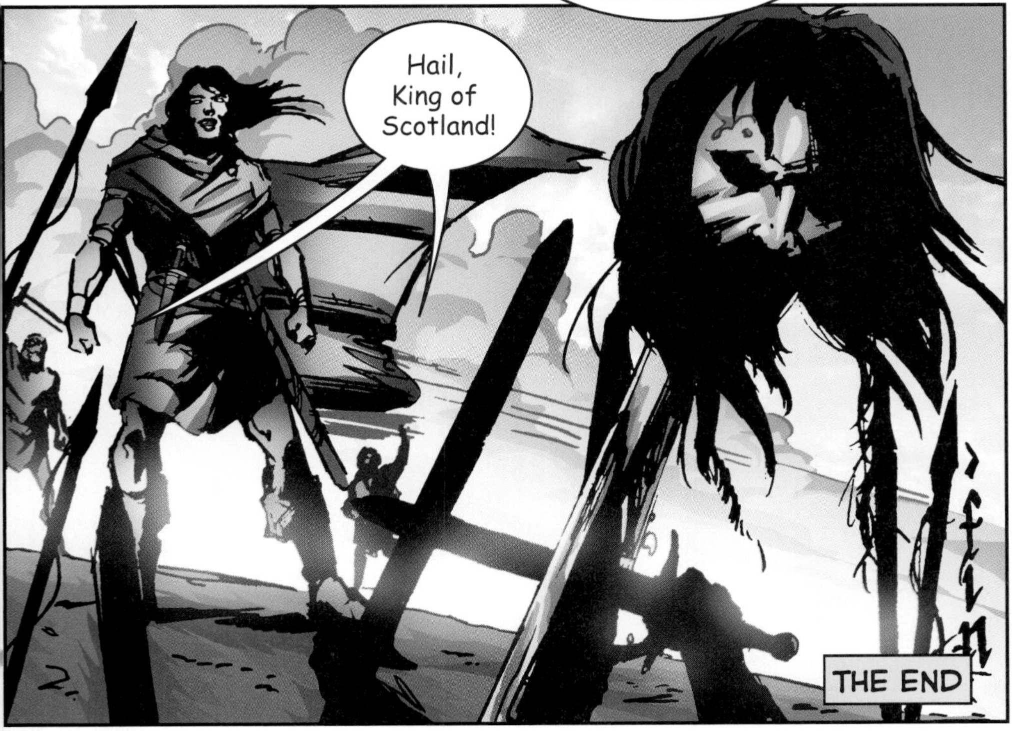
Hail, King of Scotland!
fin
THE END

WHAT SHAKESPEARE WAS SAYING

Sometimes when you hit a difficult phrase in Shakespeare, all you need is a translation. But sometimes you need a bit more—an explanation of what's going on.

page 8, panel 1: *When the hurlyburly's done, when the battle's lost and won.*
TRANSLATION: When the chaos of the battle is over.

page 8, panel 1: *Upon the heath. There to meet with Macbeth.*
TRANSLATION: On the heath. There we'll meet with Macbeth. (A heath is a large, wild area of grasses, ferns, and heather.)

page 10, panel 3: *The Thane of Cawdor lives. Why do you dress me in borrowed robes?*
TRANSLATION: The Thane of Cawdor is alive. So why are you calling me by his title?
EXPLANATION: If someone is wearing "borrowed robes," he's pretending to be someone else.

page 11, panel 2: *Yet do I fear thy nature. It is too full of the milk of human kindness to catch the nearest way.*
TRANSLATION: I think you're much too kind to kill the king.

page 12, panel 1: *Thy letters have transported me beyond this ignorant present, and I feel now the future in the instant.*

TRANSLATION: Your letters have allowed me to see what will happen in the future.

page 12, panel 4: *Screw your courage to the sticking-place, and we'll not fail.*

TRANSLATION: If you summon up enough courage, we won't fail.

EXPLANATION: When turning a screw, there's a point at which the screw is firmly in place and will not fall out.

page 14, panel 1: *Is this a dagger which I see before me? Come, let me clutch thee. I see thee still, and on thy blade and dudgeon gouts of blood, which was not so before. There's no such thing. It is the bloody business which informs thus to mine eyes.*

TRANSLATION: Am I actually holding a dagger? I imagine that I see blood on the blade and handle, which was not there before. But it's not really there. What I plan to do is so awful it makes me imagine this.

EXPLANATION: Macbeth is so anxious about killing the king that he imagines that he's holding a dagger covered in blood.

page 15, panel 3: *Sleep no more! Glamis hath murder'd sleep.*

TRANSLATION: Thane of Glamis, you will never be able to sleep again.

EXPLANATION: A voice has told Macbeth that the murder will haunt him.

page 18, panel 2: *There's daggers in men's smiles.*
EXPLANATION: Malcolm suspects that people are pretending to be his friends but really want to kill him.

page 22, panel 5: *It is concluded: Banquo, thy soul's flight, if it find heaven, must find it out tonight.*
TRANSLATION: It is decided: Banquo, tonight you will find out if your soul is destined for heaven.
EXPLANATION: Banquo will be killed tonight.

page 24, panel 1: *Near approaches the subject of our watch.*
TRANSLATION: Here's the guy we've been waiting for.

page 26, panel 3: *If I stand here, I saw him. Avaunt! And quit my sight! Let the earth hide thee! Thy blood is cold.*
TRANSLATION: If I stand here, I can see him (Banquo's ghost). Get out! Get out of my sight! Go back to your grave. You are dead.

page 30, panel 4: *Macbeth shall never vanquished be until great Birnam Wood to high Dunsinane hill shall come against him.*
TRANSLATION: Macbeth will never be beaten until Birnam Wood moves to Dunsinane.
EXPLANATION: Macbeth's castle is on Dunsinane hill. Birnam Wood is a forest several miles from Dunsinane. So it seems impossible that Birnam Wood could ever move to Dunsinane.

page 30, panel 5: *Then live, Macduff. What need I fear of thee?*

TRANSLATION: Then I won't have to kill Macduff. I have no reason to be afraid of him.

page 34, panel 5: *Let grief convert to anger. Blunt not the heart, enrage it.*

TRANSLATION: Turn your grief into anger. Don't dull your feelings; make them stronger.

EXPLANATION: Malcolm is telling Macduff not to lose himself to sorrow, but to turn his sorrow into anger and seek revenge against Macbeth.

page 37, panel 1: *Out, damned spot! Out, I say! Who would have thought the old man to have had so much blood in him?*

TRANSLATION: I wish that bloodstain would go away. Who would have thought that Duncan would bleed so much?

EXPLANATION: Lady Macbeth is haunted by the murder of Duncan. She thought she could forget it, but she can't stop thinking about it. She feels guilty. Now all she sees is his blood.

page 37, panel 2: *She has spoke what she should not, I am sure of that. Heaven knows what she has known.*

TRANSLATION: Lady Macbeth has talked about something she should not have discussed. I hate to think of what she has done.

page 37, panel 3: *Unnatural deeds do breed unnatural troubles. More needs she the divine than the physician. God forgive us all! I think, but dare not speak.*

TRANSLATION: Terrible actions bring about terrible troubles. I think Lady Macbeth needs God's help more than a doctor's. I suspect that she has committed some terrible crime, but I don't dare voice my suspicions.

page 38, panel 2: *Now does he feel his secret murders sticking on his hands.*

EXPLANATION: The knowledge of all the evil and killing that he has done is tormenting Macbeth.

page 42:
> *Tomorrow, and tomorrow, and tomorrow,*
> *Creeps in this petty pace from day to day*
> *To the last syllable of recorded time,*
> *And all our yesterdays have lighted fools*
> *The way to dusty death. Out, out, brief candle!*
> *Life's but a walking shadow, a poor player*
> *That struts and frets his hour upon the stage*
> *And then is heard no more: it is a tale*
> *Told by an idiot, full of sound and fury,*
> *Signifying nothing.*

TRANSLATION: Tomorrow always comes. We cannot stop time. And no matter how much a person thinks he controls his life, he has no control over its end. So what does it matter what we do in life? We all die. Real life is of no more value than the pretend life of an actor on stage. The actor performs his scene and then leaves. He has affected nothing. Off the stage, we think ourselves to be important, but in the end, we too have changed nothing. Existence has no meaning.